Secrets of SEO Marketing:

Strategies on How I learned to Get to the Top of Search Engines and How You Can Too

By Jimena Cortes

Copyright 2011 by Jimena Cortes
All Rights Reserved.

Reproduction or translation of any part of this book beyond that permitted by Section 107 or 108 of the 1976 Copyright Act without permission of the copyright owner is unlawful. Requests for Permission or further information should be addressed to info@wizardmedia.net.

Table of Contents

Preface……………………………………………5

Chapter 1: How I Learned SEO ………………11

Chapter 2: Understanding the Search Engines and Searcher Behavior……………………………16

Chapter 3- Keyword Research.. …………………24

Chapter 4: Defining Your Goals……………34

Chapter 5: On Page SEO……………………39

Chapter 6: Your Blog and/or Forum……………47

Section 2: Link Building………………………53

Chapter 7: Creating and Distributing Articles……57

Chapter 8- Videos and Podcasts………………67

Chapter 9: Press Releases……………………74

Chapter 10- Blog Commenting and Links………78

Chapter 11: Directories…………………………84

Chapter 12: Forum Posting……………………92

Chapter 13: Social Bookmarking………………95

Chapter 14: Social Media……………….……..…...98

Chapter 15: Tying it all together……………….…101

Chapter 16- SEO Q&A………………………...…..113

Chapter 17- SEO Tools……………………….….117

Chapter 18- Tips and Tricks for Your Website…..119

Preface

I wrote this book for those who know nothing about SEO and want to learn true and proven strategies to get their websites to the top of the search engines. This is not an advanced book on SEO, but rather more of a beginners guide to understanding how it works. Can you put the strategies in this book to use and see great results? You bet, but SEO is a process in which you need to be consistent and patient. Over the next few chapters I will share with you the secrets of SEO that I have learned to rank any website I want in today's biggest search engines like Google.

Over the past decade, the World Wide Web has integrated itself as a large part of our societies and everyday life. It has created Billionaires out of some, multi-millionaires out of others, and countless jobs. It has also created new industries and most importantly new ways to connect with prospects even for offline businesses.

However, many businesses have been rather slow to react to these changing times. If you have already created a website and put your company online, congratulations! If you have yet to make that leap, do not worry, armed with this book you will learn what you need to know about attracting qualified customers to your site. Actually, it may even be to your benefit if you have not created an online presence yet.

The reason being that this way you learn what you need to do first, so you can complete this task with a clearer plan of action that will save you many mistakes that I had to learn by costly trial and error.

My reason for creating this book is to help business owners recognize the huge opportunity they have to attract customers when they leverage the power of the search engines. Now there are two ways to get traffic from search engines. One is through pay per click, such as Google Adwords. The other, is by being listed organically in their search results.

The problem with paid listings is that in many markets you can be paying anywhere from $1-$5-$25 or more per click! And when your budget runs out, so does your ad. Another draw-back is that people know those listings are paid, so they tend to click on them less than the organic results, which they deem to have more authority since the search engine ranked them.

PPC is a great strategy to attract customers, however you must look at it as more of a short term marketing strategy and SEO as a long term marketing strategy. The reason being is that you can put up an ad today and you can start getting clicks and calls tomorrow. And that's great about it. However, as time goes on and more advertisers with larger budgets start coming in, your cost per click is going to continue to rise, making it more difficult and expensive to compete for the same terms.

Typical Clickthroughs on SEO vs Paid Search Ads

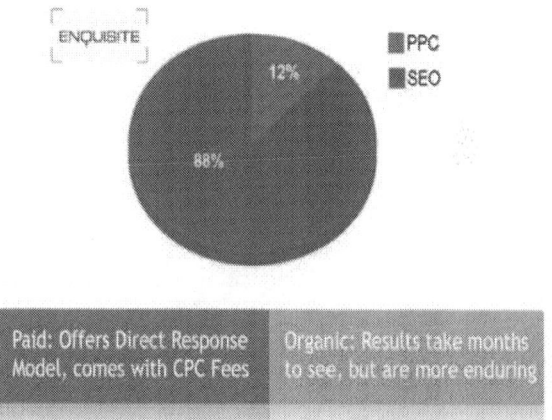

With organic listings your site always comes up when the keywords you rank for are typed and you pay nothing per click.

However, just because you don't pay per click with organic traffic, it doesn't mean it's "free". It takes a lot of time and effort to get your site to the top and time is money.

However, the benefits of SEO are much greater since it gives your site a reputation as a credible source, because search engines like Google are highly trusted. If you're number 1 for a term, then people tend to assume you must be the top company/expert in that field.

With a good SEO strategy you can bring a high amount of targeted visitors to your site who see you as an authority just because a search engine listed you on their first page of results. This is why this book is dedicated to helping you do just that.

What I see when I talk to business owners is confusion as to where to put their marketing dollars so that they actually get a positive return. There's a lot of options out there of where to advertise, and many slick sales people will show up at your door selling you ways to advertise, whether it be a directory, a magazine, newspaper, TV, etc but can they guarantee that people who need or want what you have to sell will see the ad? Chances are the answer is no. This is why search engine optimization is such a powerful and effective way to advertise your business. The only people who find your site will be those who are looking for the products and services you sell. Once you have attracted these qualified customers it is up to you to make sure that your website sells your stuff better than the competition. If you do SEO properly and you have a website that converts well, you will be on your way to creating a profitable business, one where do you don't have to wonder where the next client or sale is coming from because you get them daily from these efforts.

That is the power of SEO, which is why I have devoted my career to not only mastering this valuable skill, but also helping others grow their business with it. I can't think of a more rewarding feeling than knowing that I can literally turn around someone's business for the better by applying these skills properly. These skills have taken me years and a lot of money to learn and I will be covering my SEO secrets in the following pages.

It is by no means a mistake that you found this book. This book is going to help you grow your business and understand and master an otherwise mysterious and confusing skill: SEO

Even if you don't do your own SEO after you have read this book, you will understand how it works, so that if you decide to hire someone to do this for you, this book will give you the ability to ask the right questions, and know what the person you hire should and shouldn't do. Unfortunately there are a lot of bad SEOs out there that give this industry a bad name, and it's a shame. However, when you know this stuff yourself, it will be much more difficult to take advantage of you.

That's actually how I learned SEO, but I will be covering this information in the following chapter more in depth. Now back to marketing online. I am amazed at how many entrepreneurs I talk to who don't even know what kind of return on investment they are getting from the little bit of marketing they are doing. Others when they start to track, often times will see that the money they are spending does not pull its weight. The days of putting an ad in the Yellow Pages and waiting for the phone to ring are long gone.

Other forms of advertising are on their last legs and losing their effectiveness. For example, newspapers are declining rapidly in readership, with TiVo consumers can now fast forward through your commercial, the do not call list stopped many telemarketing campaigns (and if you ask me telemarketing is interruptive, a primitive form of marketing, and not a good experience for the sales person or the prospect), Direct mail can work, but often times you will get a 1-2% return and the cost of postage continues to increase, print ads also have rising costs, and emails most of the time either get blocked or don't get read, since people are now bombarded by emails.

With all these obstacles, can you think of a more powerful marketing strategy than being found on the number one position on Google, Yahoo or Bing when your prospect is searching for a solution to their problem and your product or service is the one they need to solve it?

I don't think so. The power of having a proper SEO campaign is the equivalent of having a Billboard on Times Square and everyone who looks at it are people who were looking for what you have to offer at that exact moment. This book is designed to help you understand how to implement a proper SEO campaign and understand how the search engines work. After reading this book you will be prepared to take on the search engine giants.

One thing to note however, search engines like Google are constantly changing their algorithms so what works in SEO today, at the time this book is being written may not work as soon as 1 year from now. To stay abreast all of the constant changes in search engine marketing, you can visit my website at www.wizardmedia.net and read my blog or look for an updated copy of this book on the site. Also, it is a good idea to sign up for my monthly newsletter where I discuss the latest in SEO and marketing related information.

Chapter 1
How I learned SEO

This will be a rather short chapter, but an important one nonetheless. I want to share with you my journey and how I decided to learn this skill. Everyone's way and reasons for learning are different; mine came disguised as a misfortune.

In mid 2009 I decided to launch a self defense products website. Since my background was in marketing and I knew how much advertising costs via direct mail, magazines, TV and PPC, I knew there was no way I could be effective in these media with the limited budget I had. I knew in my heart that being able to rank at the top of Google for terms related to the products being sold in the store would be my ticket to making this business successful on a shoe-string budget.

At first, I tried to learn SEO myself by visiting marketing forums online and reading blog posts. I thought because I came from a marketing background and had experience with online marketing that this would be easy. That could not be further from the truth. I spent countless hours trying to figure out the SEO giant.

There seemed to be so many conflicting opinions online about all aspects of search engine optimization. The more I "learned" the more confused I grew.

People were suggesting all kinds of ways to rank your site and trying to sell you their product to get you to the top. With so many options and conflicting information I just had no clue what to spend my time doing for best results, how to do it properly, how to track it or where to put my money.
After 6 months of trying to optimize my site on my own and getting nowhere, I decided that I would hire a company to do it for me.

An Indian firm named Auroin called me up, and ran reports on my website that looked very professional.

Because of the professionalism they showed me, the low enticing pricing they gave me and the big promises they made, I decided to hire them for a 3 month campaign. We agreed on 10 keywords that I really wanted to rank for at the time and paid my fee of $400 per month. They even offered me a special promotion of 10 additional man hours per month if I signed up by a certain date. I took their offer.

After the 3 months, they told me if I was not ranked for the keywords we agreed upon, they would continue to work free of charge until I was on page 1 for my chosen terms. I thought this was a win-win situation, so what could possibly go wrong?

They sent me monthly reports on the progress of the campaign, showing me all the book marks and links they got for me. They helped with some of my on-page SEO, although looking back now at what they did and what I know, it wasn't the best. They did article marketing the first month, which I knew should be a part of the SEO campaign because it is to this day very powerful.

They then told me to continue the article marketing for the second month there would be an additional fee. Oh oh, looks like red flags are starting to show up, besides the fact that they are in India…

So three months came and went, and I was still nowhere near page 1 for any of the terms we chose. On 1 term, I was on page 7 and that is the closest I got. All others I was not even in the top 100 results. The most that this company did for me was taking my page rank from 1 to 2. If you don't know what page rank is, don't worry, I will be covering that in later chapters.

So naturally, I thought ok whatever, this will take longer than I or they originally thought. Just as a precaution I canceled the card they had on auto bill so no funny stuff happened in month 4.

As you can probably imagine, they were not willing to stand by what they promised, and came after payment for month 4 if I wanted to continue the campaign, so obviously I did not. I realized I had just lost $1200 and all I got from it was a page rank that was a little better and on page 7 for 1 term.

No increase traffic whatsoever which is what I was going after. So it was back to square one. Now I was forced to learn SEO. I wrote down all the tactics I had read about online. I tried out several techniques and tested how effective each was. I finally started to see a significant boost in my rankings and in my traffic. Soon I started to get sales.

I had cracked the code. I read blogs, books, bought digital courses and frequented marketing forums tirelessly; I took the things that confused me or stuff I had found conflicting opinions on and just tested it. I saw results. I was so happy that now my website was making money and I had learned a priceless skill. I now had the power to rank websites at the top of search engines and get floods of free targeted traffic to any site I wanted to. I felt on top of the world and I was.

If this company had never stiffed me, I would have never learned this skill. I would have never found my calling. After I learned SEO, it was great that I had a successful site, but I realized that I really enjoyed doing this work more, but most importantly I enjoyed the results it gave the people I was doing it for.

A proper SEO campaign can take a business on the edge of bankruptcy, back to success. Your customers, no matter what business you are in, are searching for you online, and online reviews are the new word of mouth.

If you don't believe me take a look at what you do. When you are looking for a product or service, do you use the internet to find what you need? Do you find several resources for that product or service and then based on many different factors like website professionalism, price, credibility etc, make a decision on who to buy from? Do you ever research a company before doing business with them and if you see bad reviews think twice before handing them your money or walking into their location?

I bet you do, and guess what, your customers do too. So if you ignore having an online presence, you are ignoring the media by which customers find you. In the following chapters I am going to teach you everything I do to get my own websites and my client's websites to the top of the search engines. What you are about to learn took me countless hours of frustration and loss of money to figure out. I hope you enjoy this book and I hope you are able to increase your bottom line from what I am about to reveal to you

Chapter 2
Understanding the Search Engines and Searcher Behavior

As of January of 2009 according to Comscore more than 12 billion searches were being done every month online which is nearly 400 million every day, meaning that is about 4500 searches happening every single second! Before the internet people used to have to down to the library and search through countless volumes to get an answer to their questions, which now they can do in mere seconds with the power of the internet and the organization of the search engines.

When a person does a search online, they are looking for an answer, a solution or piece of information. They may be looking for a specific website (navigational query) to buy something (transactional query) or simply to learn something (informational query).

We will cover these more in depth in the following pages. People typically search for phrases involving 2-3 words. If they don't find what they are looking for within the first or second page, they typically change the search query.
So you can get an idea of the market share each search engine has, take a look at this graph:

US Search Engine Allocation (January 2011) - Source: ComScore

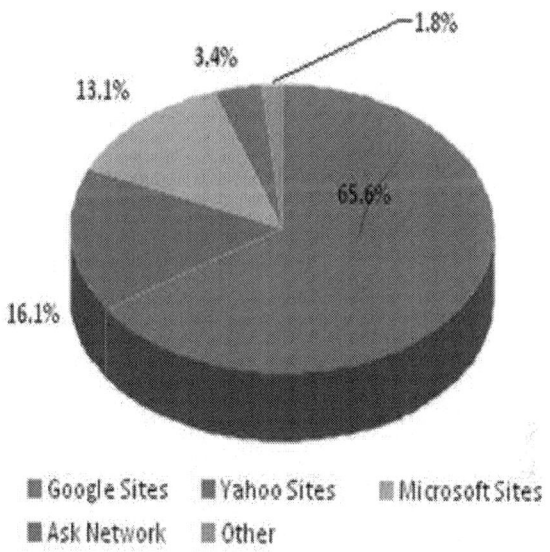

■ Google Sites   ■ Yahoo Sites   ■ Microsoft Sites
■ Ask Network   ■ Other

Search is so big it is one of the top online activities people do, even bigger than social networking believe it or not. Check out the chart on the next page:

Over time, search and email are most popular online activities

% of internet users who do each activity

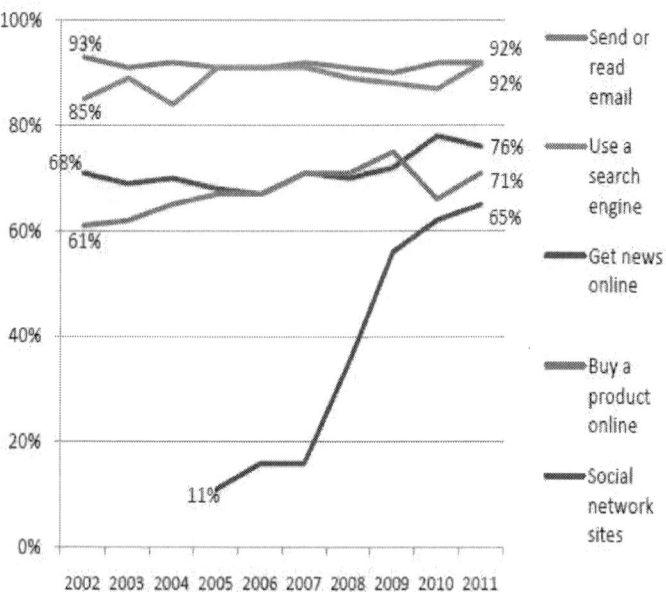

Source: The Pew Research Center's Internet & American Life Project tracking surveys, 2002-2011. Social network site use not tracked prior to February, 2005. For more activity trends, go to pewinternet.org.

There is no question that one of the best and most important ways to reach consumers and build your business is through search marketing, no matter how big or small your company is or what target market it focuses on. Now let's look at the opportunities we have to capitalize on the three different types of online searches.

Navigational Queries: (trying to find a pre-determined site)

Opportunity- pulls the searcher away from the site they are trying to find and get traffic destined for a competitor. Value- low, with the exception of navigational searches for the brand the searcher was looking for, as these will have a high conversion rate.

Informational Queries: (Looking for particular information) these types of queries are usually not transaction oriented and people may be looking for all kinds of things like the weather, directions to a friend's house, Hollywood gossip and so on.

Opportunities- if you have good information you could attract a large following or inbound links from others linking to your site.

Value- low, unless the information being searched is information on a product, service or company, then these can have high value.

Transactional Queries:
Opportunities- Achieve a transaction, whether it is a free trial, email address or actual purchase.

Value- Very high. These are the best types of phrases to go after in an SEO campaign since you will gain leads or sales from the traffic you attract.

One thing I'd like to point out, just because transactional queries have the highest value it does not mean you should rule out ranking for information queries. If your site has good information, this can be a great way to start a relationship with users who find your information useful and come back to buy from you at a later date.

Eye Tracking: How People View Search Results

Back in 2007, on SearchEngineLand's blog (http://searchengineland.com/eye-tracking-on-universal-and-personalized-search-12233)

I saw a study that caught my eye. When searching online, users spent the most amount of time looking at the top left hand corner of the search results (indicated by A). They then scan vertically from there to the titles that catch their attention the most.

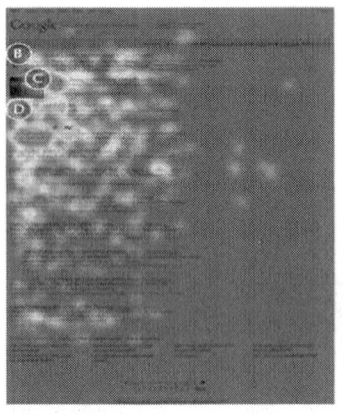

Aggregate heat map from searches for "Harry Potter" 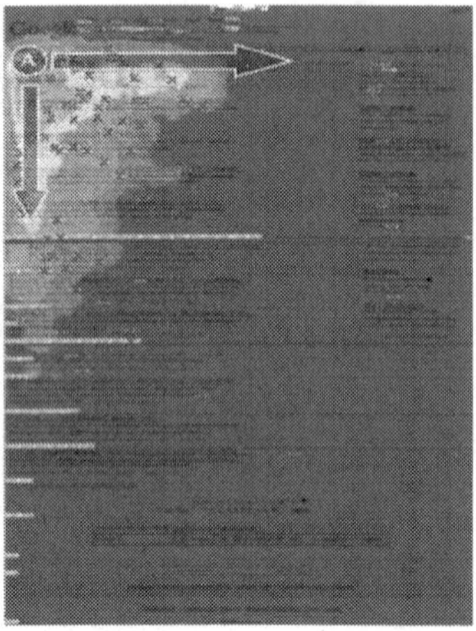   Aggregate heat map from Eye Tracking Study 2006

This is a great reminder of how important it is for a business to not just be found on page 1 of the search results, but be in the top 3 spots on the page to get the most traffic.

What Search Engines Look For

Search engines use hundreds of different factors when determining where to place each site on their search results. We will cover a few of the most important ones in the following paragraphs in no particular order.

1. **Website loading speed.** Google in particular takes into account how fast your website loads. They are obsessed with speed and want to provide their users with search results ultra fast. If you haven't noticed, often times when you search for something on Google it starts pulling up results as you are typing, as well as giving you suggestions for what key phrase to type. Therefore, if your website is slow to load this can actually affect your rankings in a negative way.
2. **Page structure.** We will cover this in more detail in the following chapters but it is a very important ranking factor.
3. **Fresh content.** Google does not like static sites that never change. If you put up a website and then never update it, to the search engines the site is static and can have negative effects on your rank. This is why it is a good idea to create a blog on your site and update it at least once a month, so that you always have fresh content. The more often you have new content, the more often the search engine spiders will visit your site. This is a good thing, so make sure to do this.
4. **Age of domain.** The older your website is the better. Often times it is difficult to get a new website to high rankings because it lacks domain age. The best thing to do in this scenario is purchase your domain for several years, so the search engines

can see that you are not a fly-by night spam site and you plan to stick around. Then be patient, as your road to high rankings will be longer than a website with at least 1 or 2 years of being around.

5. **Social Media.** As of 2009, search engines including Google, Yahoo and Bing started tracking social media interactions into their algorithms. This means that now your social media status can affect your search engine rank. The more followers, friends, re-tweets, fans and interactions you have in your social media accounts, the more that is going to help you in ranking for your keywords. Be sure to be active in social media and link your accounts to your website.

6. **Text on page.** This should be an obvious one, but it is amazing to me how many people don't write the page text on their websites without their keyword phrases in mind. How are you going to rank for "SEO company" if that phrase is nowhere on your page? Make sure not to keyword stuff that phrase either. Just put the keyword phrases your want to rank for naturally on your page. Keyword density should be around no more than 2%.

7. **Title tags, Meta tags, description tags and alt tags.** These in a sense go along with the text on page description I mentioned above. You want to put your keywords in the title of the page, not the name of your website as I see many people doing. The same goes for the other tags, but we will cover this with more detail in the chapter titled "On-page SEO".

8. **Bounce rate.** The bounce rate refers to how long someone stays on your site before they "bounce". If your site visitors land on your page and then stay on for a few seconds before they leave, chances are

you will have a high bounce rate and this will have negative effects on your SEO campaign. Google wants to deliver great results to its users, so if your website has a low conversion rate and high bounce rate, your site must not be very engaging, and thus you will be listed lower in the search results.

9. **Back links.** This is one of the most important ranking factors to this day, and the bulk of any SEO campaign. Getting other websites to link back to yours is like getting a vote for your site. The more people who "vote" for you, the more popular the search engines think you are the higher they will list you on their results. Not all back links are created equal. Some carry more weight than others. For example, if a high authority site like CNN.com links to you, their link can count for as many as 1000 links from lower quality sites. We will cover this topic in more detail as well in the following chapters.

Chapter 3
Keyword Research

Keyword research is the most important part of any SEO campaign. If you choose the wrong keywords to target, all the on-page SEO and link building in the world is not going to make you any money. Remember, the whole reason you are doing any of this is because you want to make money. So if you choose keywords that are not profitable for your business, which only bring traffic that is not targeted, then everything else will be a waste of time.

If there is any chapter in this book, you really need to master, it would be this one.

There are many tools you can use for keyword research. To keep things cost effective for you, I will focus on free tools.

When you first begin this step, think about who your ideal customer is. Think about the most profitable products and services you offer. The ones you want to sell the most of.

Then, think of the possible keyword phrases customers would type to find those products and services or your kind of business.

Create a list of these types of phrases. If you sell several products or have several services, create several search phrases for each you think people might type to find this.

For example, if you are a contractor, someone may type contractor, roofing contractor, plumbing contractor, etc.

Then take into account geography. Are you a national business that sells products locally, nationally or internationally? If so, you probably only need to rank for the products and services you sell like "diamond rings" for example. But if you are a local business, then you want to rank for what you offer within the city which you service.

Going back to the contractor example, you may want the keyword "contractors in Las Vegas" or "general contractors Las Vegas" if that is where you do business.

Also take into account motivation levels and desires. Someone may want to find the best in the business so they may type "best contractor in Las Vegas" or "top personal coach". You need to consider all of these possibilities when creating your keyword list. To keep track of the terms you want I would suggest creating your list in Microsoft Excel.

Now that you have your keyword list ready, put some of the keywords into the Google insights for search tool found here:

google.com/insights/search

When you put your keyword terms for a particular product or service here, you will see the search trends over time of those phrases. Why is this important? Because we do not want to focus our SEO campaign on terms whose search volume is decreasing. This free tool will also show you the top searches related to what you put in and rising or "breakout" searches. Pay attention to the rising searches listed and the top keywords listed as well. This is a great tool to get ideas on additional keywords to research, since it is giving you the top terms and those that are rising in search volume. Add the keywords from this list to your excel sheet if you find some that you'd like to possibly target.

Repeat this step for all the products and services you have. Make sure you add the recommended terms you want from here into your saved keyword list. We then want to check how much traffic they have.

We can do this by using Google's keyword tool. To find it, just type Google keyword tool into Google and it should be the first result. Put all the terms you want to check in here. You can only put up to 100 phrases at one time to check.

Once you do that, Google will show you how many monthly searches each phrase has. They will also suggest additional keywords based on what you put in.

On the left hand side of the page, you will see something that says "match types" and it will say "Broad", "Exact", and "Phrase". I typically choose exact, which I means I want to see the exact amount of searches for each phrase as it appears exactly. If you choose to view the broad traffic for example, it will show you the amount of searches made with any of the keywords in the phrase in any order.

I don't like to look at broad traffic personally, because some people type things like "free" or "cheap" with the search term I want, and that's not the traffic I want to include in my search numbers. The reason being because I will not be targeting that kind of traffic since they are not looking to buy. Broad match is too broad and I want to see the traffic for that particular search phrase, not for all possibilities with those words in it.

Phrase match means you are viewing all the searches with that particular phrase in it, but will include searches with additional keywords.

When you see the search traffic with the exact match, now you can see which phrases or keywords are the ones with the most traffic. Remember, these search numbers are only for Google, which means for each term there actually are additional searches being done in either Yahoo or Bing. However, since Google has the majority of the market share, that additional traffic is rather small.

You can click on the keywords that most interest you from this list and download it onto your computer. What I like to do at this point is check the amount advertisers are paying on Adwords for the terms I am interested in. You can do this by switching to the "Traffic Estimator" tab on the left hand side of the page. Also, you can sign into Adwords with your Google account and it will show the cost per click in the initial search without having to switch to the traffic estimator.

I do this because if someone is willing to pay more for a particular term than another, that means that term is probably converting better for them.

Once you hone in on the key phrases with the rising or top searches, a good amount of traffic and a high CPC (Cost per Click), you have a list of potential great profitable keywords to target.

Now you have to determine how difficult or how competitive the websites are in the top positions on Google for this term. This is competition research and will be covered more in depth in the following section.

Competition Research

Type the keywords you are researching into Google one by one. Look at what websites come up first. Take the URLS of the top 3 sites and put them into www.woorank.com

This website will help you analyze the top sites for the term/terms you want and let you see several important key factors to show you why they are the top site for that keyword.
Factors such as what did they put on their title tag, meta tag and keyword tags, you won't know why this matters just yet, but we will cover these things in detail in the next chapter.

You also want to see how many back links they have. Keep in mind that this tool is not 100% accurate on back link information. I have yet to find a tool that is, but it will give you a good idea of how much optimizing a competitor has done. Back links are still a huge ranking factor for search engines as we've already covered. If a website has a lot of back links, it is a more competitive site to go against than a website who has very few. Sites with optimized titles, Meta tags, keyword tags and a lot of back links, particularly if these links are from high quality sites, will be difficult to out rank.

Not saying impossible, but if your website is brand new especially and this is your first SEO campaign you are doing, you want to target terms for your campaign in which the competition isn't as steep.

As you are doing this competition research, I suggest taking notes either in a notebook or on a word document, so you can keep track of what sites are number one for the terms you want and how competitive they are. Write down how many links they have and what keywords they are targeting on their website with the following instructions.

Now just because a website has a ton of links, and it is listed in the top for the term you want, it does not mean it is a really difficult site to outrank for that term. I know it may seem that way, from the previous paragraphs, but let me show you how to know.

Go to that website, and right click it with your mouse. A menu will pop up and you will select view page source:

This will show you the code of the site. At the very top you should see a tag that says: `<title>` and then some words next to it. If the keyword or phrase you want to rank for is not in the title, then this would be an easy site to outrank even if it had thousands of back links. Same thing if you do not see the keywords in the Meta description tag below or the keywords tag which is below the description tag. However, if you do see that they are clearly targeting the keyword you want on their page, they are ranked well for and have thousands of back links, this would be very difficult to outrank just starting out. When this happens it does not mean it is impossible to outrank them, it will just take more work, and a lot of time and patience.

Here is a photo of how these tags look on the next page.

```
<title>Self Defense Products | Women Self Defense | Surveillance Security</title>
<meta name="Description" content="Self defense products - browse through our large selection of powerful self defence to keep you and your family secure." />
<meta name="Keywords" content="self defense products, women self defense, surveillance security, pepper spray, stun g
<meta name="googlebot" content="all" />
<meta http-equiv="Content-Language" content="en-US" />
<meta name="robots" content="noodp" />
<meta name="slurp" content="noydir" />
<meta name="revisit-after" content="1 days" />
<meta name="robots" content="index, follow" />
<meta name="no-email-collection" value="http://www.myselfdefensestore.com" />
<meta name="Reply-to" content="support@myselfdefensestore.com"/>
<link rel="canonical" href="" />
<meta http-equiv="Content-Type" content="text/html; charset=iso-8859-1" />
```

This always appears at the top of the page. A cool thing about doing SEO is sometimes a website with a lot of back links and good on-page SEO will rank for certain terms that they were not even optimizing for, just because they discuss it a little bit on their site and that term is not very competitive. If this is a term you want, and you come across this situation, then this is good for you because it will be easy to outrank them as long as your site is more focused on this term both on page and off page. We'll talk about off page SEO in a few more chapters.

Another tool you can use to see where your competition got its back links is www.backlinkwatch.com. It won't show you all of them, but it will give you a good idea of what sites link to them, so you could try to get back links in all of those sites and additional ones as well to outrank the competition. After all, you only need to be a little bit better than whoever is at the top to beat them.

We will cover off-page optimization in further chapters in section 2 of this book and then the reasons why you are looking at these metrics will make more sense.

Other things too look at would be the age of the top sites for the term you want. To check that information you can use the website grading tool at www.websitegrader.com. The older the site the more competitive it is. If you come across a situation where all or most of the websites on page 1 for a keyword have been around for several years, this could be tough. However, if they are not well optimized in back links or on page factors then this could be good.

You also want to take a look at the page rank of your competitors, the higher this number is the more difficult things can be. If you are a brand new site, it would be tough to outrank a website that has been around for 5 years and has a page rank of 4.

You may be asking, well what is Page Rank? Page rank is a link analysis algorithm named after Larry Page. It goes from 1-10, with most good sites being around a 3 or 4. Sites with high page rank above 5 or 6 are usually very well known big sites. To give you an example, cnn.com has a page rank of 9, Bloomingdales.com has a page rank of 6, and Facebook has a page rank of 9. This is an indicator you can use to see how "authoritative" Google deems a website to be. To see this metric, just download the Google Toolbar on your browser and click to display Page Rank.

Once you've analyzed your competition, choose the top 5, 10 or 15 terms you want to go after. Remember, these have to be terms that are rising in search, have some of the higher cost per click you found, are relevant to what you offer, have a good amount of monthly searches, and the competition is beatable. Don't target broad terms.

In SEO you may hear something called "long tail keywords" which are key phrases that are several words and more specific. When starting out it is often better to target long tail keywords because those would be easier to rank for than shorter terms. For example, getting to page 1 for the keyword "real estate" would be much more difficult than "real estate homes for sale in Las Vegas". Plus, a long tail keyword is more specific so the searcher may be more willing to buy at this point rather than a person conducting a broader search.

Last thoughts:

When you're choosing the keywords your website will target you should always bear in mind the adage "less is more". Sometimes selecting the keyword that will bring you the most traffic is not always the best option for your business, in fact it could be a big mistake. This is because it could be a difficult term to rank for and/or it could bring you a lot of traffic, but no buyers. You are doing SEO to make money, so don't get stuck on just getting traffic, you need traffic that is willing and ready to buy.

Always start out optimizing for at least five keywords. If you optimize your website for just one keyword, not only are you narrowing your market but you're also waving a big flag to the search engines saying, "Please Penalize Me". Remember, search engines don't like SEO – they don't like people manipulating the results. If you target only one keyword it will be very obvious that you are performing SEO on your website and chances are you'll be penalized as a result.

If you have a new website, the chances are your website will be "sand boxed for several months for any popular keywords. So if you target your website solely for the most popular terms in your niche then your website won't even appear in Google's search results (due to being sand boxed) for several months and the competition for such a popular keywords is typically very tough, so getting a good ranking will be difficult. It is always better to have some traffic as opposed to no traffic. This is why it is sometimes better to start with long tail keywords and then work your way up to more competitive terms, once you have some solid rankings.

Do this right and you are on the right track to have a very profitable SEO campaign. Read over this chapter several times if needed, this is one of the most important steps in the process.

Chapter 4
Defining Your Goals

After you have done your keyword research, competition analysis and honed in on the keywords you want to target, you need to set goals for your campaign. SEO is a very specialized task and it is a marketing function of your business. Search engines have the power to drive a high amount of targeted prospects to your site who are looking for your type of product or service. Therefore, it is very important that you set specific goals and objectives which can be measured. If your goals cannot be measured, then they are not useful.

Setting these objectives will help you determine whether you are getting a good return on investment from your SEO campaign. Whether you are doing it yourself or paying a professional to do it, it will cost you either time, money or both, so you want to make sure that this time and/or money is well spent.

First, you need to view this campaign correctly. If you view SEO like pay per click, which is something you can turn on and off at will depending on budget, is like seeing exercising as something you do when you gain weight, as opposed to having a healthy exercise routine weekly. With SEO, those who will see the biggest benefits are those are patient and committed. SEO is something you continually do once you start.

Now let's talk about your branding goals as they relate to SEO. Often consumers assume that because a website is ranked highly in the search engines, it must be one of the top in their industry. If you use the search engines quite regularly, you probably know this assumption is not true, however many people still do.

Traffic to your website is obviously one reason you want to do SEO, so think about your expectations in this regard. Talk it over with your team as to how much increase in traffic you would like to see. Have realistic goals, this is very important.

Traffic and branding are great, but the real reason you are doing this is because you want to increase sales, leads, or ad revenue. The awesome thing about SEO is that it not only gives you more traffic and a reputation increase online, but also it delivers TARGETED site visitors who have an interest in what your business has to offer. This is why a well designed SEO strategy can result on a very high ROI when compared to other marketing methods.

Consider how much you want to increase sales. Again make sure your expectations are realistic. An SEO professional should be able to help you with this task if they know what they are doing. If you don't know your goals just yet, I sometimes like to come up with this part of the plan after I do the initial keyword research which we are going to cover in the next chapter. The reason being, after I do that research I have a better idea of how much traffic I can expect and based on that I can know better what I should shoot for.

The great thing about setting goals is that if you fall short, you can tweak your website or SEO efforts to deliver you what you need. If you supersede your goals, then you can create new ones to grow your online presence.

Here is an example of how I may define my goals after I have done the keyword research (which will be covered in the

Let's Talk Numbers

Here is a screen shot of a local niche: Moving Companies in Los Angeles.

Keyword	Competition	Global Monthly Searches	Local Monthly Searches	Approximate CPC
[moving services los angeles]	High	170	170	$14.08
[best moving company los angeles]	High	36	36	$14.90
[moving company los angeles]	High	590	590	$14.26
[moving companies in los angeles]	High	480	260	$15.32
[hollywood moving]	High	46	46	$9.15
[los angeles movers]	High	1,600	1,300	$13.61
[hollywood movers]	High	210	170	$11.84
[beverly hills movers]	High	170	170	$11.28
[los angeles moving companies]	High	720	590	$15.30
[hollywood moving companies]	High	< 10	< 10	$11.35
[movers beverly hills]	Medium	58	46	$12.90
[movers hollywood]	High	58	58	$14.12
[best movers los angeles]	High	28	22	$13.23

Keyword	Competition	Global Monthly Searches	Local Monthly Searches	Approximate CPC
[hollywood moving companies]	High	< 10	< 10	$11.35
[movers beverly hills]	Medium	58	46	$12.90
[movers hollywood]	High	58	58	$14.12
[best movers los angeles]	High	28	22	$13.23
[best moving companies los angeles]	High	22	22	$14.91
[house movers los angeles]	High	16	12	$11.87
[moving companies los angeles]	High	1,000	1,000	$14.43
[movers los angeles]	High	1,900	1,900	$14.52
[moving los angeles]	High	260	210	$11.92

If you were to rank on page 1 of Google for the terms listed above, your site would have shown up in **over 6,602 searches.** Now let's be conservative. Pretend you were able to get 10% of that traffic to your site.

That would give you **660 new visitors every month** who are looking for a moving company.

If you paid for that traffic, on average you would spend about $14 per click bringing the total to **$9,240 per month** to have that many people come to your site.

If you convert 10% of your traffic to leads that is **66 new leads every month.**

If 25% of those leads convert to paying customers and your average customer value is $1000, then that would bring in an additional **$16,000 per month to your business**. Are you starting to see the power of SEO? Are you also starting to see how you can gauge numbers and put real tangible goals in place for your campaign?

If you start getting that kind of traffic and it is not converting like you hoped, then you need to make changes to your website to convert the traffic coming in better.

Chapter 5
On Page SEO

Now that you have chosen the right keywords for the campaign, we need to make sure the search engines see your website as the authority for the terms you want to rank for.

The first thing you want to make sure you don't do is build a website all in flash. These are not search engine friendly, although search engines have made great advancements in technology, this site will be much more difficult to rank.

If you must use flash on your site, that is fine, but make sure you have pure html text on the page as well. Flash should only be maybe one banner at the top.

Many people today are using Wordpress as a template to build their websites. Wordpress has a lot of plug-ins you can use and have an SEO friendly site structure. If you haven't built your site yet, this may be a great option to start with. Another great thing about Wordpress, is that they have a very user friendly interface.

You also want to have SEO friendly urls. Here is what I mean by that: Take a look at http://www.myselfdefensestore.com/Taser-Gun.html you can clearly see that this page is about taser guns, from how the URL looks the same goes for all other products and categories. If they had their URL look like this: http://www.myselfdefensestore.com/T8226pa?ge.html then that is not an SEO friendly URL.

While we are discussing urls, if you want to rank even faster for a particular term, having a keyword rich URL really helps. For example let's say you really want to rank for "diamond rings". This is a very competitive term, but if your website address is www.JPDiamondRings.com it will be 10 times easier to rank for that term, than if your web address is www.JPjewels.com

You will probably rank for phrases with the word jewels in it much easier however. I have done this several times with sites. Before I even buy my domain name, I do my keyword research and figure out which words I want to rank for the most, then I try to find a keyword rich url I can use. This saves me a lot of time SEO wise. The only site I did not do this for was www.wizardmedia.net. The reason being I want my brand in my URL and I was less concerned with keyword rich URLs, although I am optimizing my site. However for smaller sites where I am just looking to do a few sales a day of a particular product, then I use keyword rich urls so I cut my work load for SEO on that site.

Now let's talk about your **title tags**. The title tag is what you see in the browser as the title of a website. Search engines put a lot of weight on what your title tag says. Though it is not so visible to a human on the site, a search engine looks at this tag to tell it what the site is about. So if you want to rank for a particular keyword, it must be in your title tag. Your title tag should not be any more than 60 characters long, so do not over stuff too much text here as I see a lot of people doing and also don't under use this either. Try to fit about 60 characters with as many keywords as you, can that you are targeting for this page.

A huge mistake I see many people doing is putting something like their company name, URL or worse a phone number in their title tag. The title tag should be used for your keywords, if you want search engine traffic. However, if you plan to rank high for your number or company name then I guess putting them on the title tag is ok. Just kidding.

If you do not know where the title tag is, I explained it in the previous chapter. To implement I suggest giving the text you want for your title tag to your web designer.

The key to successful on page keyword optimization is to optimize your pages for a relevant keyword patterns, not just a single key phrase. So how should you choose these 'Keyword Patterns'? Let's assume you want to rank highly for the terms "jewelry" and "diamond rings" – both of which are highly competitive terms as these keywords generate a lot of traffic. I would combine these 2 terms so that they created several out of them. How? Easy, I would put in my title tag for example "fine jewelry and diamond engagement rings for sale".

These words should be used in my title, in my description, in my keywords tag, and in my body text of the page in a natural manner. Using a combination of this phrase in some form within the title is a must if I want the search engines to see that my website is very relevant for these keywords.

Doing this gives me the potential to rank well for a wide variety of phrases like jewelry, jewelry for sale, fine jewelry, engagement rings, diamond engagement rings, diamond engagement rings for sale, rings, rings for sale, diamond rings…. and so on. Are you starting to see how that 1 phrase can help me rank for a variety of keyword phrases?

As discussed earlier, the **title tag** should be no longer than 60 characters, so use your keywords wisely so the phrases you put here can actually create a wide variety of keywords. Using the jewelry example I may do something like this:

Fine Jewelry and Diamond Engagement Rings for Sale| Las Vegas

The reason I put the keyword Las Vegas at the end, is because I am perhaps a local jeweler and want to drive foot traffic into my store. Therefore people looking for any of the keyword combinations this creates in Las Vegas could find my site. Some keywords this would make include:

jewelry,
 jewelry for sale in Las Vegas,
fine jewelry Las Vegas,
Las Vegas engagement rings,
Las Vegas diamond engagement rings,

diamond engagement rings for sale in Las Vegas and so on. I would also perhaps rank if these words were typed without the city name after my site gained some authority. Ranking in local markets is much easier than nationally. Obviously there is more competition for the term "jewelers" than "jewelers Las Vegas" since there are fewer jewelers in Las Vegas than in let's say the entire U.S.

Next, we want to create the description tag also known as the **Meta tag**. This is the description that shows up in the search engines when you make a search and a see a small paragraph next to each result. For this, you want a short paragraph no more than 160 characters and we want to use keyword patterning here as well. A description for the jewelry example may go something like this:

Johnson Jewelers is one of the best jewelry stores in Las Vegas. We carry a wide selection of diamond engagement rings, watches, necklaces and more. Click Here.

I want to do several things with this description, I want to create as many possible key phrases as I can, and also sell the prospect on clicking on my listing vs. the competition. This is exactly 160 characters, so the prospect with see the whole thing, including the call to action which is "click here".

I also added additional keywords that I could possibly rank for such as jewelers, and jewelry store do you see that?

Last but not least, we have the **keywords tag**. We want to put no more than 10 keywords here separated by commas. For this example, our keywords tag may look like this:

jewelry, jewelry for sale in, fine jewelry, Las Vegas, engagement rings, diamond engagement rings, diamond engagement rings for sale, jewelers, jewelry store

These keywords are not visible on your page to your visitors, but the search engines read them and that's who you are doing this for. Take this process and repeat for every page on your site. Make sure you make your tags are relevant to what the page is actually about, and you are not just putting keywords for the sake ranking for them.

All of your pictures have an attribute called the alt tag. You should incorporate your keywords in them. For example, if you have a picture of a ring on this page, name the **alt tag** "diamond engagement ring" as that is one of our keywords and will help our page seem more relevant for this term.

Don't name all of your pictures the same. Play with the words a bit. You have plenty to choose from hopefully.

If you don't understand how to place these tags, your web developer should know. Just write the text out for them and tell them where you want each tag placed. Most developers or web designers don't fully understand SEO, so often times they will put nothing in these tags. It is up to you to be proactive and tell them what text you want placed there for best SEO results.

So now what we need to do is create the page content and an internal linking structure that will compliment the keyword patterns. Remember, I'm not targeting the phrase "fine jewelry and diamond engagement rings for sale", but rather different variations of the words that are in this phrase, so all I need to do is create pages that are optimized to contain these words.

Since I'm not targeting one specific phrase over and over, there is no chance of the website appearing to be "spammy". Rather, it will make my website appear to be very natural to the search engines without any blatant SEO seeming to take place. In many instances, just having a good linking structure and well-written unique content on your site, will be enough to get a good ranking for some niche keywords that will bring highly targeted traffic to your website. This is of course, if they are not highly competitive terms.

When I mention linking structure, you want the most important pages at most 1 click away from the homepage and you want to place anchor text links with the keywords you want to rank for within the text of your site. For example, if one keyword is "diamond ring" in the text of my site I want to put an anchor text link to the page about diamond rings with the anchor text "diamond rings" leading to it. If you don't know what anchor text is, I will be explaining it more in detail in Chapter 6.

Make sure the text that goes in each of your pages is unique; search engine don't like duplicate content so it is very important to have original content you or someone you hired wrote. Be careful if you are a retailer and just copy and paste descriptions and titles of products from the manufacturer. You should make those titles and descriptions unique as this will greatly help your SEO efforts. Make sure the content is quality content and has a keyword density of 2%, no higher.

Keyword density refers to how much you use a particular keyword on the page. If you use it too much, you run the risk of being spammy. To check this, you can use the following keyword density checker:

http://tools.seobook.com/general/keyword-density/

Chapter 6
Your Blog and/or Forum

Back in Chapter 2 we discussed what search engines look for on a site. One of the things they like to see is fresh content. Having a blog on your site is going to help create that "fresh content".

I suggest you update your blog at least once a month, but ideally if you can do twice a month or even once a week that is best. Make sure the content in your blog is unique, meaning it cannot be found elsewhere because you have not posted this content elsewhere to avoid duplicate content penalties.

You can incorporate a free blog into your site very inexpensively. Just ask your web designer or developer to incorporate a free blog like Wordpress into your site. If you are using a third party service like Wordpress or Blogger for your blog, make sure you are not hosting it with them.

There reason being, your blog URL should look like this: www.yoursite.com/blog and should be easy to find from your homepage. Not, wwww.name.wordpress.com. The reason we want to do this is to make sure when you make updates to your blog, it counts as an update to your website.

Having a blog is great for having fresh content, plus you get to share your thoughts and expertise .It also helps you develop a relationship with your site visitors. This way, you don't constantly have to update your website either to have that much needed fresh content.

When you write blog posts, I use suggest linking back to your site with anchor text links. What does that mean? Well let's say one of the pages on your site focuses on diamond engagement rings. So you write a blog post on the last engagement rings that came in. Within the post you put a link back to the diamond engagement rings page, but instead of the link saying "click here" the link says "diamond engagement rings" since that is a keyword we are targeting.

When a search engine spider crawls your post and follows that link back to that page, the anchor text is letting it know that the page is about "diamond engagement rings" and not about "click here" as many links usually say.

To further prove this point, go online and type click here into Google.

You can see from the search results that Adobe is the top result. Why? Because there are so many links to their products online that have the anchor text "click here" that they are the authority in the eyes of Google for this term.

So when you make a post on your blog it is good to have 1 or maybe 2 links pointing back to your main site with the keywords that you want that page to rank for. Here is an example from my blog:

You can see I am linking back to my homepage, with the anchor text SEO firm.

If you don't like blogging, you don't always have to make your own blog posts either. You can invite others to contribute content to your blog in the form of articles, videos and pictures.

If you link to 3rd party sites in your blog or articles on your site, make sure to put a "no follow" tag on the link so that you do not pass your link juice to them. Also, don't like to competitors, you wouldn't want to send them your potential customers.

Creating Anchor Text Links

So far I have talked a lot about anchor text links, but haven't showed you how to do it; well here is the html code you need to put on your site or 3rd party site to create the link:

<a href=" http://www.yourwebsite.com"> Your Keyword</a>

Sometimes 3rd party sites have a link generator to help you link a particular keyword to a site, if it's available I suggest using that, but if it's not, this is how you can create the link yourself.

Creating a No Follow Tag

You can use no follow on individual links by simply typing rel="nofollow" after the link in the href tag. A typical link would look like:

<a href="http://thisIsJustAnExampleLink.com" rel="nofollow">Your anchor text here.</a>

That's all there is to it.

Forums

Another tactic you can use to have fresh content regularly on your site and engage your audience is implementing a forum on your website. This is a great thing to do instead or along with your blog. People love to discuss things in forums related to subjects they are interested in or things they need help with.

For example, if you are a chiropractor, you can implement a forum on your site and start some discussions related to questions your patients always ask. If your patients are always asking these questions, then it is very likely these are questions your site visitors will have.

The cool thing about forums is that people need to register in order to post there, so this is a way for you to collect contact information from your site's visitors you may not have not otherwise received. You can use those email addresses to stay in touch with your community members and offer them special deals at your practice.

Another example is if you have an e-commerce site and you implement a forum, this can be a place where you discuss uses for the products, people can ask questions about the products or share their stories about using them and how it made a difference in their lives. Again, you can use the forum as a way to get people's contact information and follow up maybe once per month via email.

Forums are very easy to implement on your site and there are some platforms that are even free to use their forum template. The only cost you would incur would be the cost to have a developer connect the forum to your site and this can be done rather inexpensively.

To have a better forum template than the free ones with fewer features, you might pay $10 or so a month to use the platform, but this is still better than paying to develop one from scratch.

Section 2: Link Building

Now that I have taught you how to optimize your website pages, it is time to start the meat of the SEO work, which is the off-page optimization. Up until this point, you have learned keyword research, how to optimize your website for the keywords you want to rank for, by putting in the correct titles, meta tags and description tags. Also by having an SEO friendly site structure and a blog you update regularly for fresh unique content.

You have also learned about some of Google's ranking factors which include the on-page stuff, like site speed, conversion rate, bounce rate, age of your site and other factors. However, having all those done right, don't guarantee high search engine rankings. The fact of the matter is that all of that stuff counts really for about maybe 40% of the work. But to this day, even with Google's recent Panda update and constant algorithm changes, one of the biggest factors affecting how high you rank is still incoming links.

Link building is a fundamental part of SEO, and unless you have a super powerful brand that attracts links without you doing much, then your SEO campaign will fail without a proper link building strategy.

This is especially true if you happen to be in a competitive market. Links are like votes for your website. If site A has 1 incoming links and B has 500, site B seems more popular so it will in theory have better rank than site A. Incoming links are just sites that link back to your website.

Not all links are created equal however. Some links carry more weight than other links. For example, if I get a very authoritative site like CNN.com to link back to my site, that link would count the same as 1000 links from lower quality sites.

How do you know if a site is really authoritative? Check their page rank.

How do you get a higher page rank? Get more incoming links and grow your traffic. Now I am not going to get into the specifics of page rank, but just know, the higher the page rank, the more that link is worth to you from that site.

For example, one link from a Google Page Rank (PR) 5 page is equal to getting 555 links from Google PR1 pages. Now that's what I call link juice!

Just because low page rank sites don't carry as much weight as higher ones do, it does not mean you should not also get these kinds of links. First of all, they are much easier to get, and second of all you want your link building to look natural. If only high page rank sites link to you, then the search engine crawlers may think that is a red flag and "unnatural". This can give you away and in turn your links could be devalued.

Instead, work to get links from both low and high page rank sites, which will look more natural. Remember, search engines do not want you to manipulate their search results, so when you do an SEO campaign, you want to stay under the radar. Having a "natural" link building campaign is the key to maintaining your rank. After all, you are going to work very hard for it, so it would be devastating to lose all of that hard work.

Another thing I want you to remember is that you want to get 1 way links to your site. A lot of sites will say they will give you a link if you give them one back, but that is like giving someone a dollar and them giving you one back, it doesn't do much.

As you can see, 1 way links are more powerful, so I will focus on showing you ways to get 1 way links.

Sometimes it is ok to do 2 way links, but that is only for sites you are maybe partnered with and want to show them on your site as they do the same for you. Don't use this as a tactic for link building though. Otherwise you won't get very far in the search results.

In the following chapters, I will be covering several link-building strategies I use to get high search engine visibility.

Make sure you read every chapter and especially the chapter about "Tying it All Together". You don't want to go out and just get a bunch of links, especially all at once, so be sure to read that chapter and preferably this book entirely so you do every piece of this correctly. This information took me 2 years to learn and perfect, you are getting the Cliff notes version and bypassing much of my trial and error. So be sure to pay attention and implement as explained here.

Chapter 7
Creating and Distributing Articles

Besides unique blog posts, you need to create additional content to promote your site online. Content is a great way to establish yourself as an expert and get tons of incoming links! What kind of content should you create besides of course regularly updating your blog?

Articles
Videos
Press Releases
Podcasts

Articles:

For this section of the book, we will focus on articles. Create articles that target 1-2 key terms from your list. Write the article with valuable and quality content. If you place the article on your site, don't place it elsewhere because remember Google does not like duplicate content.

An article should be informative. Good articles leave the reader knowing something they didn't know prior to reading. People read articles expecting to either learn something or be entertained—you should try to aim for both.

Articles can vary in length, from a few paragraphs to many pages. How long your article is depends on the information you're trying to convey. For SEO purposes, I normally like to keep articles anywhere between 400-500 words. You are welcome to make them longer, but it just creates additional work, and when you are doing this on a weekly or even daily basis as I do, 500 words is plenty to get your point across.

Do not use articles as blatant advertisements. This is a crucial concept many webmasters fail to grasp, but one you should learn if you are trying to use articles to increase site traffic and sales.

Now that you know what articles are, let's talk about why you want to take the time to write them. Ask any successful internet marketer the secret to getting website traffic and earning repeat visitors/customers, and you will often hear, giving valuable content, which develops a relationship with their audience.

Articles are content that give substance and value to both visitors and search engines. Once your website has content, you're on the road to search engine visibility. By offering your visitors something of value, you not only increase the chance that they'll come back, but also that they will tell friends about your site

How to write a great article:

Now you need to know how to create a great article. Internet articles generally have three parts:
- Title and/or subtitle
- Body text
- Author's bio, credentials, and **links**

Remember, the goal of the article is not to sell a product, but to give away useful information to the reader. The body text of an article should not be a commercial for what you're trying to sell.

You can write an article on just about any topic you have knowledge of, as long as you can relate it in some way to your website and your products or services.

Here are some examples of different types of articles you can create:

• **How-to:** This is one of the more popular types of articles to write. If you can show your readers how to do something they have questions about, this will help them get their questions answered, and help you look like an expert.

• **Opinion:** No matter what industry you work in, there are always breaking developments, new products, people to comment on, etc. You can write an article focusing on an emerging aspect of your business, and offer your opinion on how it will affect the industry.

• **Personal story/inspirational essay:** Pretty much all business owners have a compelling reason they went into that particular business. Consider writing an article or articles about why you chose the path you did. You can try to make it humorous, or inspirational, or both. Human-interest stories are a popular article format and something I did in the beginning of this book. Although I don't think I made it very funny, maybe I should work on that.

• **Book excerpt or condensation:** If you're selling a book, e-book or e-course and you have articles built in to your product, you can give your website visitors a free sample chapter, or write a condensed article based on one of the ideas in your book.

• **lists.** A lot of articles are centered around a list concept .It can be a top 5, 10, 20 or any number you choose; For example, one list article can be" Top 10 Things Everyone Should Know About SEO."

If you are having writers block, here are some resources you can use to research information on the topic you want to write about.

Wikipedia – www.en.wikipedia.org: This free online encyclopedia contains over one million searchable articles on various topics.

HowStuffWorks – www.howstuffworks.com: A comprehensive searchable website that explains "how everything works. Categories include people, science, health, entertainment, computers, auto, home, money and more.

Fact Monster – www.factmonster.com: Another searchable database that features an online almanac, dictionary, encyclopedia and atlas.

RefDesk.com – www.refdesk.com: This site indexes and reviews web-based resources and archives quality informational websites.

Ezinearticles- www.ezinearticles.com: An article directory site I often use to get ideas on what subject to write about for my next article. There are thousands of articles here on nearly all topics; you should be able to find something related to your niche.

The Title

The title of the article should be compelling, which is why how to and top 10 lists for example make great titles. Look at how magazines or news papers do their titles. They draw you in by saying something you may want to know the answer to. For example, which of these articles would you prefer to read?

1. "Using Proper On Page SEO"

Or

2. "The Biggest SEO Mistake Most Business Owners Make and How to Fix It"

I would guess the second one right? Do the same for yourself.

Use one of the keywords you are trying to optimize your website for in the title of the article. You should also use that keyword a few times within the article body as well, but don't overdo it, otherwise you risk looking spammy.

Links within your articles

For articles that are going to be placed on your site, you are welcome to put links within the body of the article, either to pages on your site where readers can find further information on what you're talking about, or you can link to other sites who can be valuable resources to your readers. If you do link to outside websites, make sure they are not direct competitors of yours and you place the no follow tag on the link.

For articles that you are going to submit to other sites, like article directories for example, make sure that you follow that particular site's rules about putting links within the article. Some places allow you to put link in the article, others only in the article resource box. I normally do no more than 2 links in my articles, in the article resource box, to different pages on my site with the anchor text for the keywords I want to rank for in search engines.

Article Resource Box

At the end of every article, you should include a short bio of who you are, which establishes you as an expert, and a reprint disclaimer. These things help establish your credibility on the subject, and direct readers who find your articles on other websites to your site. Make sure when you direct visitors to your website, that you use anchor text links in the bio, for the keywords you want to rank for. This is one of the main reasons you are going through the trouble of creating an article. One is to get traffic from it and establish yourself as an expert, and the other is to get links from the sites where you place your articles, back to your site with the correct anchor text. This is going to tremendously help your search engine visibility.

Your bio can be short and to the point, no more than 2 or 3 sentences. Here is an example of one I might do for myself:

"Jimena Cortes is a search engine optimization expert, who has been doing SEO and internet marketing for several years. Her SEO Company helps many businesses get qualified leads from search engines and increase their bottom line."

The words I highlighted in blue would be my anchor text links. I am not currently targeting those keywords for myself; I just wanted to give you an example.

Reprint Disclaimer

All articles you write should include a disclaimer giving people the right to repost and redistribute the article on their own websites. Be sure to state that in your bio and signature file or you won't be able to take advantage of inbound links and additional traffic their reposting your article could give you.

Your disclaimer should read something like this:

This article may be reprinted or distributed in its entirety in any e-zine, newsletter, blog, or website. The author's name, bio and website links must remain intact and be included with every reproduction.

This ensures you will be given credit for the article, while allowing others to use your content without contacting you first. Most webmasters don't want to take the time to contact authors for permission, and are more likely to reprint articles that allow them to repost without much work except giving you credit.

I have an article that I wrote several years ago, which another webmaster took and posted on their website. They gave me the credit and put my links at the bottom, and I not only get link juice from it, but on average about 200 visitors a month to my site. Not bad for an article I wrote once.

Posting Your Articles

To get traffic and links from your articles I recommend posting them everywhere you can online. Below is a list of the top 50 article directories you can post to. There are many others out there and if you do a Google search I'm sure you can find additional ones. However, posting it to 50 directories should be enough to start.

knol.google.com
ehow.com
squidoo.com
ezinearticles.com
hubpages.com
examiner.com
articlesbase.com
technorati.com
seekingalpha.com
associatedcontent.com
buzzle.com

suite101.com
gather.com
goarticles.com
brighthub.com
ezinemark.com
helium.com
selfgrowth.com
pubarticles.com
articlesnatch.com
articlealley.com
ideamarketers.com
thefreelibrary.com
sooperarticles.com
infobarrel.com
amazines.com
bukisa.com
selfseo.com
triond.com
articledashboard.com
web-source.net
articlerich.com
isnare.com
articlecity.com
articleclick.com
articlecompilation.com
articlesfactory.com
submityourarticle.com/articles/
articleblast.com
searchwarp.com
articletrader.com
upublish.info
xomba.com

articleslash.net
articlecube.com
EvanCarmichael.com
biggerpockets.com/articles
snipsly.com
articlesnare.com
informationbible.com

Aside from article directories, you can start to develop relationships with other bloggers and ask if you can contribute content to their blogs. This is a win-win situation because the blogger gets new content for their readers, and you get 2 things; a link back to your site from the author resource box, or maybe even within the article if the webmaster allows and you get traffic to your site from that blog's audience. This is a very good way to get both traffic and links.

Chapter 8
Videos and Podcasts

I recommend using video marketing in any online campaign you do. People love to watch videos, and normally prefer them over reading a web page. YouTube is also the 2nd largest search engine, so that says something about how much people search for answers to their questions or just entertainment via video search engines.

If you have a commercial, and want to post it on video sharing sites that is fine, but try to make videos that follow the same guidelines as the articles. Try not to be a blatant sales pitch, but rather be informative and drive viewers from the video site to your site to get more information on the topic. Videos are a great way to not only get free traffic, but also a great source for back links.

Unlike article sites, most video sharing sites do not allow you to put a link back to your site with anchor text, but you can put a link back to your homepage url within the description of the video. This is how you can get link juice from video sharing sites and help your viewers find your site once they watch your video.

Creating the Video

First let's discuss the making of the video. One way to create a video is to take the article you wrote and narrate it on PowerPoint. You can use tools like Jing, for example that cost only $15 per year to help you create short videos.

When you use Jing, you can't make videos longer than 5 minutes, and it basically captures what you are doing on screen, so if you take your article, put it in PowerPoint, and read it as you go through the slides, there's your video. With this tool you can then upload that to YouTube or get the MP4 of it and upload it to other sites as well.

Another tool you can use is animoto.com. This is a more advanced video making tool than Jing, but they allow you to add cool effects to your video to make them look nicer and more professional. Some features of this service include:

Adding images
Adding royalty free music
Unique background styles
Unique features to make your video text or pictures fade in

And much more. They have a free version, as does Jing, and the paid version is only $5 a month. There are other pricing plans but I suggest you choose what is best for you.

Another option is to use video editing tools, if you are savvy at using these, which I will admit I am not. Or if you really don't want to bother with this at all, you can hire a professional to create the video for you.

Whichever route you take, making a video is not that hard. You can also just take a video of yourself speaking to the camera and sharing valuable information about questions your customers want answers to and post that. If you are camera shy, you can go with the options I outlined above.

Submitting the video

Once you have created your video, now you are ready to submit your video. The first thing you are going to have to do is give your video a title. You want to make the title enticing for someone to want to click on it, as well as have one of your target keywords or key phrases in it so that this keyword phrase is associated with your site even on 3rd party sites.

A good title would be similar to the ones we discussed in the article marketing section, like How to, top 10, and so on. Make sure your keyword phrase is in it! I cannot stress that enough.

Next you have the description. Here is where you are going to place the url of the homepage or subpage in your site that you want to drive traffic to for that particular video.

For example, if the video is in regards to a particular product I sell, then I want to have that keyword in the title, and then drive people to the subpage where that product is found. In this situation, I would not put my homepage in my description. I would put the subpage. This URL, is the first word in the description. After it, you write a couple of sentences describing what your video is about.

In the sentences of your description, you want to make sure you use your keyword phrase again. Make sure to use it in a natural manner.

Then, you can also put tags for your video. You want to make the tags the keywords you are trying to optimize your website for, which should also related to the video. Normally you don't want to do more than 6 keywords here.

And that's all there is to it! Here are some of the top video sharing sites I suggest submitting <u>ALL</u> of your videos to:

AOL Videos
AtomFilms.com
BoFunk.com
Eyespot.com
Flurl.com
GUBA.com
Kewego.com
LiveLeak.com
LiveVideo.com
MegaVideo.com
Motionbox.com
MySpace Videos
Photobucket.com
Pixparty.com
Putfile.com
Revver.com
Sharkle.com
Spike.com

Stickam.com
SUMO.tv
Twango.com
Veoh.com
Viddler.com
Video.google.com
Video.yahoo.com
vidilife.com
Youare.tv
YouTube.com
Zippyvideos.com

Create accounts on all of these sites and make sure every time you have a new video, it gets submitted to all of them. They are a great resource not only for traffic and exposure but also for back links. At minimum, do 1 video a month if you can. Trust me, the hard work pays off.

Podcasts

You can easily take your videos and create a podcast out them as well. We want to do this for additional exposure. Podcasting is a very popular way for people to receive information because they can consume the content in several ways.

They can listen to podcasts online, on their Iphones or MP3 players, and they can listen to them in their cars as well. Podcasts are flexible, versatile and portable, which is why a lot of people seek information this way so they have something to listen to when they drive or go for a run.

For you, podcasts are a great way to market yourself and your business because they are easy and inexpensive to create and they allow your message to be heard by many people. You can use podcasting to create relationships with people and establish yourself as an expert in your field.

When people listen to your podcast, they get to know you better. And this can be a great soft sell approach to selling your products and services.

Again, follow the same guidelines that we discussed in article marketing. You don't want to be a sales pitch, but rather a giver of valuable information. If people want more information you can invite them to visit your website.

Don't be afraid of creating a podcast. All you need is a microphone (which many laptops come with built in) and some free podcasting software.

Once you have your podcast done, you can submit it to the following sites for distribution:

AllPodcasts.com
AmigoFish.com
Blubrry.com
Digitalpodcast.com
EveryPodcast.com
Feedooyoo.com
Getapodcast.com
Odeo.com
Plazoo.com
Podcast.com
PodcastAlley.com
Podcastblaster.com
PodcastExchange.org
Podcasting Station
Podcastlikethat.com
PodcastPickle.com

RSS-network.com
Speecha.com
ThePodLounge.com
Yahoo Podcasts

You can also upload it to the ITunes store, where as you know, many people visit to download things to listen to on their Apple products.

I hope you are starting to see the power doing articles, videos and podcasts of your content can do for your business. Not only does this bring higher search engine rankings when you link your site to the content created, but also you get additional FREE exposure for yourself and business. The best part is, when you create content it stays online for years to come, so you can get traffic from all of these sources month after month, and you created the content only once.

Chapter 9
Press Releases

Press releases are a great way to get a lot of incoming links to your website as well as get visibility on news sites and even get Google rankings in as fast as 1 day!

Now these overnight rankings are usually short lived, but nonetheless you can take advantage of the traffic increase, exposure and of course, link juice.

Let me show you what I mean when I say you can get rankings overnight.

> **Real Estate** News for Realtors and **Brokers** | Inman News
> www.inman.com/
> Sep 8, 2011 – Some of those **agents** and **brokers** who are reaching out to help have been through the **real estate** wringer themselves – they may have ...
>
> News for **best real estate broker**
>
> The Real Estate Market is back in town!
> Walton Sun - 1 day ago
> Located at the far eastern end of the county, Rosemary Beach **Real Estate Broker** Linda Miller said she saw the **best** spring ever. In addition, she will have ...
> 5 related articles
>
> George Pino Leaves Flagler Real Estate
> GlobeSt.com - 5 related articles
>
> Coldwell Banker Residential Brokerage wins website award
> NorthJersey.com - 4 related articles
>
> Searches related to **best real estate broker**
>
> | | |
> |---|---|
> | best real estate **agent** | best real estate **school** |
> | best real estate **company** | best **mortgage** broker |
> | best real estate **stock** | best **realtor** |
> | best real estate **license** | 10 things your real estate broker won |
>
> Gooooooooogle ▶
> 1 2 3 4 5 6 7 8 9 10   Next
>
> Search Help   Give us feedback

I typed in the phrase" best real estate broker" into Google and at the bottom of the first page I can see the top results for news for that term. That is how a press release can get you page 1 rankings very fast. However, your listing will only last a few days, as only the "freshest" and latest news are displayed.

If you are in a market that gets a lot of press releases, then you may be knocked down pretty fast, but if that is not the case, then you may enjoy this additional traffic a little longer. Not a lot of people know about this trick, which is why it is so powerful.

But besides the visibility on news sites and Google search results, press releases can be a great way to get 1 way incoming links.

I like to use PRweb.com to do my press release submissions. They also have a great amount of resources in regards to helping you write your press release and manually review it before it goes out. If your press release is not written as it should be, they will let you know and give you tips on how to change it.

Remember, a press release is something newsworthy, so write about something new that happened in your business. Typical topics for a news release include announcements of new products, a new strategic partnership, the receipt of an award, the publishing of a book, the release of new software or the launch of a new Web site. The tone is neutral and objective, not full of hype or text that is typically found in an advertisement. Avoid directly addressing the consumer or your target audience. The use of "I," "we" and "you" outside of a direct quotation is a flag that your copy is an advertisement rather than a news release.

PRWeb is a paid service, but well worth it, since for as low as $80 your news release is syndicated to thousands of blogs and news sites across the web.

I like to use the Advanced option for $200, since it allows me to put **anchor text** links for my keywords within the press release. As you can see, this is a powerful way to instantly get tons of 1 way back links to your site.

If you do not want to submit your news release on PRWeb, you can also submit it to many free press release submission sites too. They are not as powerful as PRWeb, but still get the job done.

Below is a list you can start with:

- 1888pressrelease.com
- free-press-release.com
- prleap.com
- clickpress.com
- express-press-release.com
- prnuke.com
- prlog.org
- afly.com
- malebits.com
- pressreleasespider.com
- pressmethod.com
- pr9.net
- pressbox.co.uk
- pressexposure.com
- sanepr.com
- prurgent.com
- prfree.com
- freepressindex.com
- transworldnews.com
- prbuzz.com
- i-newswire.com
- press-base.com

Chapter 10
Blog Commenting and Links

Another easy way to get links is to comment on other blogs. When you leave a comment on a blog it often asks for your name, email, website and comment. If you put a website in that field, this will link back to your site. The name on the comment should contain your keyword. However, many bloggers won't accept comments that blatantly look like they are just trying to get a link back to their site with the keywords they are optimizing for SEO. This is what black hatters do and often times their site will get reported as spam, and they have to start all over. Don't let this be you.

Therefore if you are targeting the term "self defense products" in the name field you can put something like "the self defense product guru". Also, always make sure the comment you are leaving is quality and pertains to the actual blog post. Comments like "great post" or "such good information thank you for writing this" are generic and look spammy. Many spammers have automated tools that put comments like these in blogs and that is a sure way to prevent your link from getting approved because webmasters know this. Worse yet, your site could be reported as a spammer. Sometimes I don't even use my keyword in the name field; I just use a random name. The link will still count and my odds of getting the comment approved are higher.

If the blog does not have a field for a website, don't bother leaving a comment.

Make sure you find blogs that are at least somewhat related to your site. This increases the chance that the link will stick around for a long time, and it makes you a more valuable member of the community instead of just another spammer.

So how will you find blogs to comment on? I am about to share with you a super ninja SEO strategy I use, so pay close attention.

Ninja link Strategy:

First you want to download Firefox, if you already have it, then you are ahead of the game. Then you want to download the "SEO Quake" Firefox add-on.

For help on setting this up, check out this video on YouTube:
http://www.youtube.com/watch?v=I1Z_8xzRGwQ

Now that you have SEO quake installed, you have the tools in place to use the following technique to find blogs related to the keyword you want to optimize for.

At this point, go to Google and type in any of the following search queries to find the right blogs to comment on:

site:.com "powered by expressionengine" "ADD YOUR KEYWORD HERE"

site:.org "powered by expressionengine" "ADD YOUR KEYWORD HERE"

site:.edu "powered by expressionengine" "ADD YOUR KEYWORD HERE"

site:.com inurl:blog "post a comment" -"comments closed" -"you must be logged in" "ADD YOUR KEYWORD HERE"

site:.org inurl:blog "post a comment" -"comments closed" -"you must be logged in" "ADD YOUR KEYWORD HERE"

site:.edu inurl:blog "post a comment" -"comments closed" -"you must be logged in" "ADD YOUR KEYWORD HERE"

site:.com "Powered by BlogEngine.NET" inurl:blog "post a comment" -"comments closed" -"you must be logged in" "ADD YOUR KEYWORD HERE"

site:.org "Powered by BlogEngine.NET" inurl:blog "post a comment" -"comments closed" -"you must be logged in" "ADD YOUR KEYWORD HERE" site:.edu "Powered by BlogEngine.NET" inurl:blog "post a comment" -"comments closed" -"you must be logged in" "ADD YOUR KEYWORD HERE"

The queries from 3 to 6 are designed to find any type of blog, like Wordpress or Blogger, which are the most common blog platforms used. The other queries are for Expression Engine and BlogEngine blogs, which are both popular among academics. The reason you want to include those is to find sites with a .org or .edu URL who will let you leave a link on their blog.

Why does it matter if a site is .com, .edu or .org? .Org sites carry a lot of weight in the eyes of Google, so a link from one of these sites can be very valuable to your site even the .org site you link to has little Page rank. If you have a good amount of these kinds of links, you could very well outrank your competition sooner than you think.

To organize the results you get from your search query, you can use SEO quake to organize the sites that show up by order of Page rank. You can also organize the results by Alexa rank, if you want to leave your comment on a site that gets more traffic, thus more visibility. Overall blog commenting is a strategy I use, but not as much as articles and videos.

Articles and videos are by far what get me the best results, both in driving traffic to my site, and getting links. Google also loves quality content, so by giving them what they want, they typically reward me with high visibility in their search engine. However, because I don't want to rely on just 1 or 2 types of link building strategies, I usually sprinkle a few others in my SEO campaign. You want a variety of links from various sources. This is why I use all of the link building strategies I am sharing you in this book in almost every single SEO campaign I work on. Some campaigns are different than others, some require more work and some less, but you always want to have a diversified link strategy.

Blog commenting is a easy and fast way to get links, however its main drawback is that just because you left a quality comment it does not mean that your link will ever appear.

Webmasters have to approve those comments, so often times if I leave 10 comments, maybe 4 or 5 will actually go live. Sometimes webmasters don't even approve comments at all because they don't have the time to deal with that particular site, and I understand that as I am guilty of this for one website I built and forgot about. So don't be discouraged, just continue to leave valuable comments and you will see links come your way because of it.

To prevent spam, many Wordpress blogs come with a spam filtering service called Akismet. If this service sees that you are leaving a lot of comments on a lot of blogs all of the time, it will mark your comments as spam even if they are not. To avoid being flagged, I use a service to rotate my IP address every 30 minutes, so it looks like I am a different person. Your IP address is a unique number assigned to your computer when connected to the internet.

The service I use is Privacy Partners. Another comparable service is www.hidemyass.com.

By doing that, Akismet cannot see that my computer is leaving a bunch of comments all over the place. I also put different email addresses in the email field.

Keep track of all blog comments you leave and come back later to see if it was approved. Once you find a webmaster who approves you comments, you can leave other comments on their other posts and start developing a relationship with them. Perhaps at one point they will let you do a guest post. If not, at least you can get a few links from them since they are responsive to your comments.

Chapter 11
Directories

(This chapter is particularly important if you are a company who does the majority of business within a local market.)

One very easy way to get back links to your site is by submitting it to online directories. When you use this strategy, do not ever pay for a directory listing. Only list your site where you can list it for free.

Some directory links carry a ton of weight. For example, the best directory you can submit your site to is the DMOZ directory (dmoz.org). Search engines value this directory very highly, however it is very difficult to get your site listed here. Also, they won't tell you if your site is rejected or approved. You just have to check back.

To have the best odds at getting your link approved with Dmoz, make sure you read their guidelines and submit your site to the appropriate category. If you fail to do this, you may never get your site listed here. Be very careful before you submit your site to a specific category here and ensure there is not a more suitable one for your site. If you don't do that and submit to a category that is not appropriate, they simply just won't accept your submission and never tell you why.

After that the submission is pretty simple. For the title, enter the official name of your site. Do not add things like "Welcome to", "Home page of", or other information that isn't part of the official name. Using a keyword that describes your site name is ok as well.

For the description, enter short, objective, well-written text. Do not repeat the title in your description, do not use words like "I", "we", or "us", and do not include marketing hype. Then make sure you take note of what category you tried to list your site in and check back a few weeks later to see if you got accepted.

The only directory listing I suggest paying for would be the Yahoo directory at **dir.yahoo.com.**

The cost is $299 per year. If you don't want to spend that much, I understand and it is not a must to have this listing, but it will be in your favor SEO wise if you do. Remember, Yahoo is one of the most authoritative sites online and 1 back link from them carries *a lot* of link power.

Local Business Directories

If you own a company that does business locally you want to get your homepage listed in as many local directories that pertain to you as possible. Particularly Google places, Yahoo local listings and Bing local listings.

Claim your Google places page and add pictures, a great description using your keywords and be sure to list all of the surrounding areas you service or that you would like prospects from. Claiming and optimizing your Google places page is the most important thing you can do if you are a local business, because if you notice, when you search for a local plumber, dentist or any other local type of business, the Google place page listings is what come up first.

Take a look on the following page:

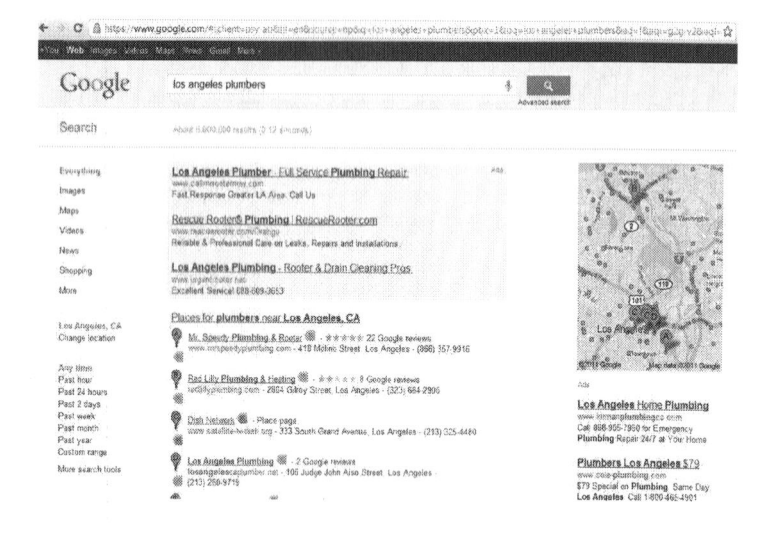

As you can see the first listings are Google place pages.

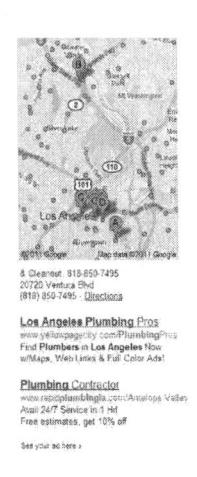

Then, below the place pages we see the regular listings. If you are a local business owner, you have the opportunity to dominate the first page of Google and be seen as the authority for your niche because of the way the listings show up. You should strive to have your place page come up first, and then have your website come up again underneath the place pages under the regular listings. If you want to be even more aggressive, you can take out an Adwords ad.

This way you are seen 3 times as opposed to once like everyone else on the page. How will you achieve so much visibility? Well the Adwords part of it is easy obviously, since you just pay for the traffic, but to rank your places page just follow all the things we are going over in this book. Over time, your authority will increase and you can very well rank in Google maps as long as you claimed your place page and drove quality links to your SEO friendly site.

As far as Adwords, I will cover that topic in a different book, for this one let's focus on SEO, but just know that this is the way you should be crushing your competition online.

To get to the top of the place pages, focus on having your customers leave great reviews about your business here. Develop some sort of incentive to get them to do so and watch the reviews go up along with your rank. Imagine how much your business will stand out if you have more positive reviews than the competition. Guess who all the business will go to? You! Take full advantage of your place page and add promotions as well as fill it out completely. Add pictures, videos and of course your website.

Tip: In the field where it says company, add your company name along with the keywords you are targeting for you homepage. Also, use keywords you are targeting for your categories to help you come up first when those are typed into Google.

Next you want to create your listing in Yahoo Local Listings as well as Bing. After these have been done, continue on to the following directories and claim your listing there if you find your business or create a new one if your business is not listed:

whitepages.com
likelist.com askdirectory.com
b2byellowpages.com
business.intuit.com
business.yellowbook360.com
citysearch.com
DaPlus.us
DexKnows.com

directorym.com
dnb.com
foursquare.com
free411.com/
GetFave.com
HelloMetro.com
Hotfrog.com
merchantcircle.com
yelp.com
Infospace.com
insiderpages.com
justdial.com
kudzu.com
LocalSearch.com
local.com/
MagicYellow.com
openlist.com
Shop.com
supermedia.com
superpages.com
switchboard.com
uscity.net
WhitePages.com
YellowBook.com
yellowbot.com
YellowOne.com
yellowpagecity.com
yellowpages.aol.com
YellowPages.com
ziplocal.com
cityvoter.com
zidster.com
shopcity.com
citysquares.com
manta.com

yellowbot.com

I typically like to also search for directories related to the site I am optimizing. When I find them I submit the site for a listing. Again I only use free directories and do 1 way links. If they require a link back from my site in order to get the listing, then I simply move on.

Finally, add your site to quality directories where they have a category for the kind of site you have. To find and submit to these directories I use the following tool: http://www.onewaytextlink.com/

If you don't want to get all these different kinds of directory links, if you are a local business, **at minimum** do the Google, Yahoo and Bing listings. But remember, these directories have traffic as well and can be a great way for prospects to find your site.

Again, never pay a directory just for a link as search engines do not value those kinds of directories and your money and time will be wasted. Here is what search engines look for in quality directories:

- If there is a fee to pay, it is for an editorial review and not for a link. Yahoo for example, gives no guarantee that even if you pay the $299 your site will be added because it may not follow their guidelines, so clearly they do reject some sites
- Editors could change your title or other parts of your listing at their whim
- Editors can reject the listing
- The directory has a track record of rejecting submissions

Before adding your link to any directory, you want to ensure that directory is of quality. Here are some guidelines for figuring this out:

- Examine their editorial policies and see if quality is important over making a buck
- Google the directory and see if they come up in the search results, if they don't, please move on
- Does that directory promote search engine value more instead of traffic? Then avoid it
- If the directories' main audience is webmasters and SEO professionals stay away from it as well

Some of the directories I listed here do have premium sponsorships, however these directories are a great source of traffic for local businesses and you are fine just using their free listings. With the SEO work you are doing you are better off not paying a premium for the visibility in their directory and spend your money and efforts on SEO instead which will pay off much more anyway.

Before you add your link to any directory you are unsure about it, make sure you do a search for them in Google. You don't want to link to a directory that has been black listed from Google. That will only hurt your site.

How will you know if they are black listed? If you search for their name and it does not show up, then they are black listed. A link from this type of directory will only hurt, not help you.

Chapter 12
Forum Posting

Forums are another great place to get links and traffic to your site. In any SEO campaign I do, I usually include some forum links. With this strategy, you want to join forums that relate to your niche. Then you want to become an active member of that forum's community.

There are several reasons for this. One, if the forum is a place where potential prospects could be, by you adding value to the forum community, people will want to know what you have to say and this can create exposure for you and your site.

The other reason is many forums allow you to add links in your signature or in your profile settings. When you add value to the community and people see your signature and click on the links which direct them to your site, this brings prospects to you. These prospects may feel as they already know and trust you because of your interactions in the forum. Also, you are getting the link juice from the forum as well so this will help in increasing your search engine rank.

Follow the same guidelines of anchor text we covered in previous chapters if the forum allows. Before adding links to your profile, be sure to go over that forum's guidelines for this and follow them. If not, you risk being banned from that forum and others for spamming.

In the image below, you see an example of a forum signature. The keywords "dog repellent" "surveillance systems" and "gps tracking" is what that person is targeting. This signature will show up in every post that user makes.

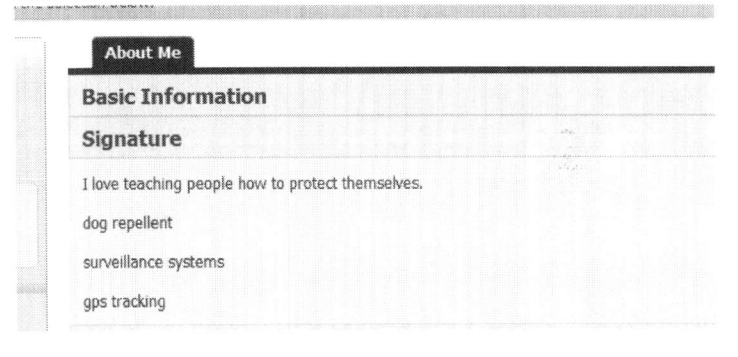

> **About Me**
>
> **Basic Information**
>
> **Signature**
>
> I love teaching people how to protect themselves.
>
> dog repellent
>
> surveillance systems
>
> gps tracking

Most forums don't use HMLT which is the kind of links I showed you in previous chapters. Instead they use BB Code. According to Wikipedia "BBCode or Bulletin Board Code is a lightweight markup language used to format posts in many message boards. The available tags are usually indicated by square brackets ([ ]) surrounding a keyword, and they are parsed by the message board system before being translated into a markup language that web browsers understand—usually HTML or XHTML."

To create anchor text in BB Code it looks like this:

[url=http://example.com]Example[/url]

In html, that would look like this:

<a href="http://example.com">Example</a>

Which makes the word "Example" link to your page.

If you just want to leave your homepage with no anchor text, then use this:

[URL]http://example.org[/url]

In html that would look like this:

<a href="http://example.org">http://example.org</a>

And to the user it shows up as http://example.org
With a clickable link to whatever page you put there.

Again focus on forums related to your niche and add value to the community. There are many programs out there that allow you to automatically create forum accounts and leave links in the signature. The problem with this tactic is it is normally short lived as most accounts will be deleted or banned since you are blatantly getting a link and not providing any sort of value to the forum. Also, forum moderators are well aware of tools like that and ban accounts that seem to be using them even if you are not.

So the best thing to do is when you join a forum, make a few posts of value and then create your signature leaving your links only if they follow that forum's guidelines.

Chapter 13
Social Bookmarking

Social bookmarking is a great way to get incoming links and sometimes even traffic. According to Wikipedia, "Social bookmarking is a method for Internet users to organize, store, manage and search for bookmarks of resources online. ...Descriptions may be added to these bookmarks in the form of metadata, so users may understand the content of the resource without first needing to download it for themselves...In a social bookmarking system, users save links to web pages that they want to remember and/or share. These bookmarks are usually public, and can be saved privately, shared only with specified people or groups, shared only inside certain networks, or another combination of public and private domains..."

When using this technique, you should always bookmark your homepage, subpages of your site that contain content and are pages you are optimizing, any blog posts you have and also book mark at least once all of your articles, videos, and press releases. This may sound like a lot of work, and it is, but bookmarking only your website is part of the process but not the entire process.

As you go out and create content like articles, videos and press releases, to make the links pointing to your site even stronger you should drive links to those pages as well. One great way to do this is by social bookmarking.

There is a semi-automated service you can use called Social Marker (www.socialmarker.com) which allows you to bookmark to over 50 different sites without having to leave their site. To save a little bit of time you can use this service when doing your social bookmarks.

The way it works is very easy. First you go to their site, and choose the sites you want to bookmark to. Then, you will fill out the information at the top with the title of the bookmark you want to post, the link (this could be to your site or one of your articles, videos or press releases) and then add a short description in the text field and the tags should be the keywords you are targeting for that page.

Once that is filled out, you click submit and it will take you to the first site to bookmark. You will first need to register for that site if you do not already have an account. Just click the register tab at the top, get signed up, and repeat this process for all the sites you would like to submit bookmarks to.

Once you have created all of your accounts, click the login tab, login, submit your bookmark and then click next at the top of the page to repeat the process with the sites that follow. The cool thing about this tool besides the fact that it is free, is that your bookmark details show up at the bottom of the page so it is very easy for you to copy and paste the information easily into the required fields.

Just because there are a lot of sites to submit to, it does not mean you need to submit to all of them, as this can be extremely time consuming, especially if you are not only bookmarking your site but your other content.

If you prefer, either hire a freelancer to do this for you, or choose the top 20 or so sites to submit to. I would highly recommend submitting to Delicious, Digg, Technorati, Reddit, Google Bookmarks, Mixx, and Propeller, but if you can do all of them, obviously that is best.

Social bookmarking should be a part of any SEO campaign. It is a very easy and powerful way to gain a link as well as exposure. I consistently get traffic from my social bookmarks, particularly from Stumbleupon.com and Digg.com.

Chapter 14
Social Media

As mentioned in the beginning chapters of this book, social media plays a role into how your website ranks in the search engines. Initially Bing came out in 2009 saying that they were including social media interactions as part of their search algorithm. Google is now also doing the same thing.

Therefore, the question is not whether you should have a social media presence or not, the question really is when will you start growing this presence and putting together a marketing plan for it, so that it not only helps your search engine rankings, but also makes you more money in the long run.

Social media marketing itself deserves an entire book on the topic. For this book, we will only focus on the part of social media which affects your search engine rankings. To understand how social media affects rank, you must first understand how search engines work. In essence, they want the most popular most relevant site at the top and then count down from there. That's why links are so important because it's like a vote for your popularity/authority.

However, if you are such an authority, then you must have a large social media following right? Well that's what search engines think. So the more social media interactions you have, the more your tweets get retweeted, the bigger your fan base, followers, views on YouTube etc the more authoritative they will see you as and in return give your website better rankings.

You must link your social media profiles to your site and also put your website link in your social media profiles. This will let search engines know that these profiles correspond to your website.

I would set aside maybe 30 minutes every day where you can focus on posting something interesting in your social media profiles and focus on growing your following.

I would also suggest you read up on social media marketing strategies, since you have to do this anyway for SEO, you might as well try and make some money from it. After all, that's the whole reason you are going through the trouble of optimizing your website.

I would also suggest having a Google Plus 1 button on certain or all pages of your site. This is still a very new feature of Google as of the writing of this book, but right now it looks like the more people plus 1 your site, the more that will help you as this is also 1 vote for your "coolness". Also, when someone who plus 1 your site is logged into Google and doing a search related to your field, your website will show up higher to them than it usually is.

If you don't have 30 minutes a day to devote to your social media campaign, I would highly suggest hiring someone to help you. This not only affects social media anymore, it also affects search, making it crucial for you to integrate both your SEO efforts with your social media strategy.

My company Wizard Media has some very affordable social media packages available. We not only focus on growing your fan base for the search engines, but also help you run engaging promotions to take your "followers" and "fans" away from the social platforms and onto your website and mailing list. And then of course, turn them into buyers.

Chapter 15
Tying it all together

Up to this point you have learned a variety of strategies to promote your site online and get high search engine rankings. However, I have not discussed with you how much to do each strategy, after all doing too little will make this take longer and doing too much could get your site penalized. So let's go over how you should manage your SEO campaign.

First you want to begin with the keyword research. This step alone typically takes me about 3-5 hours or more. I spend a lot of time analyzing every possible search phrase my tools can come up with as well as phrases I think customers would type to find the site I am optimizing. Let me repeat again, this is the most important part of the campaign. If you choose the wrong keywords all the other efforts will be wasted.

Remember to use Google Insights for search and the Google Adwords Keyword Tool to help you find the correct terms. You will be looking for search phrases that are going up in search, phrases that get a good amount of searches per month and preferably phrases that advertisers are willing to pay a premium for.

A tool I personally like to use to aide in my keyword research is also Market Samurai. I mostly use this tool to help me come up with a lot of phrases for a main seed keyword I am thinking of targeting. This tool is great for that. I also like the filtering options it has, and their competition research module. It is not necessary to use however, just with the tools Google makes available to you should be good enough.

After you have narrowed down your list some, analyze the competition and figure out which phrases will be easier to rank for. Start with those first. Leave the more competitive terms for when your site has been online longer and has more authority.

Then, once you have chosen your top 10, 15 or 20 keywords, implement the on-page optimization techniques we went over earlier. Sync your blog to your site. If you don't want to do a blog, you could also do a forum. Forums are user-generated content and can be a great way to engage your site visitors and get fresh content you don't always have to write yourself.. However, I tend to like blogs more. You are able to share your expertise better through a blog. If you want to be really aggressive, you could implement both. When you create your blog, be sure to include ways to share it. Wordpress has several plug-ins you can include on each post which make it very easy for people to share that post in other social media sites.

Next I create the necessary social media profiles needed, including Twitter, Facebook, YouTube and LinkedIn and then link them to the site. I also add a Google + button to all or several pages of a website. Be sure to brand your social media profiles with your company's color, logo and information. For an example of what I mean look at my Facebook fan page:

Also take a look at how I use the real estate I have on my wall to promote my services:

As you can see, the buttons at the top, which are just pictures I uploaded, discuss some of the main services my company provides. When you click on one these it looks like this:

In the description of the picture I put a link to my website where you can find more information on this particular service.

When you implement your social media strategy, think along these lines to make the most of the web real estate these social sites provide. It can be a cool way to interact with new possible customers.

After this has been done, you are now ready to embark on your link building campaign.

The first step here is to create the content you will be distributing that month. I like to plan on a month by month basis, you can do week by week or however you like, this is just my preference.

Typically I will create anywhere from 2-8 articles for the month per site. It really depends on how aggressive of a campaign I am working on. The more competitive the niche, the more link building I will need to do. You can put 2 back links in the article resource box, so each article will get you 2 links. In other sites, like Squidoo and Hubpages, you can add more links. I usually don't do more than 3 per article though. I make sure to place the phrases I have anchor text links for several times in the article and as part of the title. Remember it has to make sense though. Also, be sure to not overuse the terms within the article either. Using each phrase you are targeting around 3 or 4 times within the body of the article in a 400 word article is more than enough.

For a less competitive market, I will submit 1 article per week if I did 4 articles or 1 every 2 weeks if I only did 2, etc, to at least 25 directories each article. I don't do this all at once. I will do about 5-10 article directory submissions per day or so. Every article that is created should also be shared in all of your social media profiles, like Twitter, Facebook and LinkedIn. As you move forward with your online marketing campaign you should be setting time aside every few days or so at least to grow your social media presence. If you are taking 1 article and posting it in several article directories, only choose 1 of the directories to post on your social media profiles. You do not want to post the same information a bunch of times just because you put it in a different site.

I then take the article and create a short video out of it, or if you want you can create a new video. The video content I create I submit to as many video sharing sites as possible, but again only post a few each day. On a monthly basis I may only do 1 or 2 videos. I don't do video submissions for all of my clients however; some people choose to start with a more basic package which typically does not include this additional step. If you don't do videos and do everything else I mentioned, you may find you still get a good amount of traffic and good rankings, but this is a very powerful way to promote your business so I strongly encourage it.

Always post your video in the social media profiles too. Typically just the one you uploaded to YouTube will do.

Press releases I may do 1 per month or 1 every few months. I submit that to all of the sites I listed in the press release chapter and then of course I post it in all of my social media profiles. Other times I may just use PRWeb for the submission. Some people use press releases to get to page 1 of Google quickly and continue submitting press releases on a weekly basis since they don't want to do all of the other steps in SEO. I personally like to have a well diversified link strategy and only send press releases when in fact I have something to write one about.

I will do 1-2 blog posts per month to the blog on my site and share the post on social media sites for additional exposure. For my own company, I get quite a bit of traffic when I share my blog posts on LinkedIn. Especially if I do it in the groups I am a member of. The better quality your blog posts are the better results you will see.

I keep track of everywhere I post content, including all of the press release sites, article directories, web 2.0 sites like Squidoo and Hubpages, video sites, and so on. I save all of the urls that have my content and then I take those urls and bookmark them in social bookmarking sites.

I also make sure to bookmark all blog posts I create in several social bookmarking sites as well as all relevant pages on my site as discussed in the social bookmarking chapter. This may seem like a bit much, but it will make the links that point to your site from 3rd party sites stronger if you take the time to also optimize pages that link to your site. Remember, if the sites that link to you are stronger then that will benefit you more. That is why I drive links like social bookmarks to my content on 3rd party sites.

I make sure to join several forums in the niche I am in, and then become an active member in that community, perhaps visiting the forums once per week or so.

I also submit the site to as many directories that relate to my niche as possible or quality directories I find online. I don't do this all at once of course, just a few each day. Follow the guidelines discussed earlier for directory submissions. You want to make sure you don't link to directories that have low quality or whose main purpose is to sell links for the search engine value they represent.

I also comment on a few blogs each day and leave my link. Remember, you want to leave quality comments so that your comment actually shows up on the website. Check back every time you leave a comment and see if it went live. I normally check back 3 weeks later to give the webmaster ample time to read and approve my comments. Not all webmasters will approve your comments, so don't be discouraged if you check back and your comment is not live.

When you find relevant blogs in your niche who accept your comments, those are blogs you want to continue to visit and comment on other posts as well because they are responsive to you. This is a great way to also start developing a relationship with that blog's webmaster and who knows, maybe they will allow you to do guest posts as well.

I know this may sound like a lot of work and that is because it is. However, you just need to do a little bit each day. So you break it down like this:

Week 1:
- Do keyword research and competition research.
- Choose my terms

Week 2:
- Implement all on-page changes
- Create 1 blog post

- Create social media profiles

Week 3:
- Write 1 article
- Submit that article to 25 directories, doing 5 submissions per day
- Create 1 video from article or new content and submit it to 3-4 video sites each day
- Join 5 forums and make a few posts in each forum.
- Comment on 15 blogs
- Join 10-15 new directories
- Set some time aside, to login into your social media profiles, be active and grow your presence---also post your new content and anything else you feel like
- Social bookmark all pages on my site

Week 4:
- Take all content like videos and articles that are live and book mark them
- Do a few more posts in the forums and put my links in the signature or profile, depending on their guidelines
- Join a few more directories 10-20
- Comment on 10-20 more blogs
- Create podcast from Video I made or new content, whichever you prefer
- Continue to grow social media presence

Week 5:
- Submit press release to all sites you can
- Submit podcast everywhere you can
- Create another article and video
- Repeat all steps again, except keyword research and on-page SEO as that step you typically only do in the beginning (unless you decide later on to add

more pages to your site and target additional keywords)

If you continue to do this month by month you will start to see significant increases in your traffic and rank in the search engines.

This example is for a less competitive niche. If you are in a very competitive niche where your competitors are very strong sites, you will need to add more content pieces and links to this example.

You should probably set aside about 2 hours a day to do all of these tasks. It is very time consuming, but remember if you do a little bit each day that is all that matters. Don't get the same amount of links every day. Vary your numbers. Once day you might get 40, then next 10. Remember, you want to make this look as natural as possible. If you get 20 links a day 5 days a week, this does not look natural and your links may get devalued which would result in all of this being a big waste of time.

Very Important:

Ok, I had to get your attention because you must follow what I am about to say in the following sentences. I know I've stressed up until this point to have anchor text links with the keywords you are targeting pointing back to your site. However, you want things to look natural so I also suggest having several links that I like to call "junk links" pointing back to your site. Basically all these are links that instead of having your keyword as the anchor text they would have something like "click here" or "homepage" or just the web address of your site, or your company name. Naturally all of your links shouldn't be keywords you are trying to rank for, and this little trick here should help your linking campaign look more natural.

To check how well you are ranking for the keywords you are targeting you can use a tool called "rank tracker". You can use the free version and that works just fine. I typically run it once a month for each site I am working on. They have great tutorials on how to use it as well. This is instrumental in tracking your progress.

You will also notice sometimes you will climb up a lot in Google. For example, one month you might be number 15 or even number 5 for a term and then the next month completely disappear from the search results. This is completely normal in the beginning so don't get freaked out. Just continue to do what you are doing as if nothing has changed. If you stop, that's like telling the search engines you were manipulating their results and you may never come back up in the search results.

As you begin to optimize your site, you might bounce a lot in rank until you finally get to the first page and solidify your position.

Depending on how competitive your niche is you may not reach page 1 until 6 months or more down the line. In less competitive niches you may see results in as soon as the second month. Remember, be patient; this is a long term strategy not an overnight fix like pay per click.

I want to remind you that this book is perfect for those who do not know SEO at all and are just starting out. This is a good base for you to understand how it works, and how to rank your site. As you can tell this book is short and to the point. You can apply the information learned here and you will see great results.

SEO is a huge subject that is ever changing. I tried to make it as easy to understand as possible for you and kept it short and sweet. However, I do advise you to stay informed on changes in the industry. If anything, just follow my blog at www.wizardmedia.net/blog. If any major changes occur I always make it a point to make a blog post about it. You can also join my newsletter by going to my website and my newsletter has monthly updates in the world of SEO and internet marketing.

Chapter 16
SEO Q&A

If you go online you can easily find thousands of people saying all kinds of stuff in regards to search engine optimization. I actually learned SEO by buying books, courses, going online, asking questions in forums and then trying things out until I saw what worked and what didn't.

And to tell you the truth, there are a lot of people out there saying things about SEO thinking that they know what they are talking about, when in fact they are putting out wrong information. I don't know if that is intentional or not, but it happens. Therefore, don't believe everything you hear or read, test it first and then make a decision if you must find out.

So for this chapter, I want to go over some common misconceptions floating around out there.

1. **No follow links Vs. Do follow links.**

Many people say that in order for a link to count or pass "link juice" that it must be do follow. You will see this topic come up a lot in message boards. Basically what this means is that some links have what is called a no follow tag. A lot of blogs for example have this in their comments and supposedly it is so that their page rank doesn't get passed on to the sites it links to.

I see people all of the time on sites like Freelancer.com asking for x amount of do follow links to their site and I'm here to tell you do not worry about this at all. A link is a link. Plus if you have all do follow links pointing to your site, that looks unnatural and you could get penalized from a search engine. You may not be banned, but you may not rise as high as you'd like. Remember the whole point here is to have a link strategy that looks as natural as possible, so if all of your links are do follow, do you think that looks very natural?

2. That brings me to the next point, how fast should you build links?

There's a lot of confusion on this one as well. I normally build links steadily as I showed you earlier. However, when you send out a press release you might get a lot of links in 1 or 2 days. This is perfectly fine. You are not going to get penalized for having 500 links in 1 day for example, since many companies often get a lot of PR which results in them getting a lot of links at once.

What looks suspicious is if this happens only once and then never again. That's not natural. You are trying to look as natural as possible in your linking campaign, so while you may be steadily building links daily, maybe 1 week you stop but the next week you do a lot, this is fine. That seems more natural than getting the same amount of links every day, or a whole bunch one day and then never again.

3. Do all your links need to be from relevant sites?

There are a lot of people who speculate on this one, and then for some reason their theory is later taken as gospel. While it doesn't hurt to link to relevant sites, links from sites unrelated also help and count. So don't worry if all of your link partners are not in the same niche as you, as I said before a link is a link.

4. Some people say anchor text doesn't matter.

I'm here to tell you this is completely not true and anyone who says otherwise does not know what they are talking about.

5. Do reciprocal links help?

This one is one of my pet peeves. I get requests from people all of the time trying to do a link exchange and all I do is delete their email and chuckle (I'll tell you why I chuckle in just a little bit). Years ago Google actually came out and said that reciprocal linking helps you rank higher in their search engine. They posted this in their Webmaster Tools.

However, I am always very weary whenever they give out advice on how to manipulate their search engine, since they clearly state in their terms and conditions that trying to manipulate their search results is against their terms and your site could be penalized for that. Their whole purpose in their business is to have their search results be as natural as possible, so why would they tell you the secret weapon to manipulate their results?

To see who is trying to manipulate their search engine. When this statement first came out people started reciprocal linking campaigns like crazy and this spawned what are known as link farms. (Link farms are networks of people who will put your link on their site if you do the same.)

And then all of the sudden, Google changes their algorithm which they do all of the time and this was one of the things they changed. They wanted to see who was trying to manipulate the results, so many of the people who did this strategy lost rankings.

Now I am not saying not to do this all together. Sometimes you may have partners in business and you list them on your site and they list you on theirs and that's fine. Just know that those links don't carry much weight. It's like me giving you $1 and you give me $1 back. We are at the same place we started, so if you do a reciprocal link campaign for the sake of SEO, it will be a big waste of time.

Some last thoughts to finish this chapter. Whenever you hear something first think if it logically makes sense. Then, if it does, test it on a site you don't care about. Once you see your results, then implement the strategy on the "money site".

Chapter 17
SEO Tools

Let's recap some of the SEO tools we have gone over and some other ones you can use to help you in your search engine optimization efforts.

1. **Google insights**---google.com/insights/search----This will help you see the search trends over time of a particular keyword and suggest keywords who are the top for that niche and rising in search.
2. **Google Adwords Keyword tool-** adwords.google.com/select/KeywordToolExternal —This will help you see how much traffic search phrases you are considering have as well as suggest additional phrases. Use the traffic estimator to see the CPC of the phrases you want to target
3. **Market Samurai**—www.marketsamurai.com---this tool will help you with your keyword research. It is a more advanced keyword tool which also has several other features to help in your competition analysis and rank progress.

4. **Backlinkwatch**.com –This tool helps you see how many back links your competitors have and where they got them.
5. **Woorank**.com ---This tool pulls a website report so you can analyze your website better and your competitors as well.
6. **Socialmarker**.com--- This tool helps you submit social bookmarks all in one page.
7. **PRWeb**.com---This service helps you instantly submit your press releases to thousands of blogs and news related sites.
8. **MajesticSEO**.com----This is also a great tool to check the back links of your competitors.
9. **Rank Tracker**--- This is a tool I use to manage my progress in SEO rank. (do not get obsessed with checking your rankings every day, remember you may bounce around a lot especially in the beginning. Checking one a month is more than enough)
10. **Keyword density checker-** http://tools.seobook.com/general/keyword-density/
11. **Directory Submission-** http://www.onewaytextlink.com/
12. **Jing**---Screen capture software made by TechSmith
13. **Animoto**.com---Video making service
14. **SEO Quake**—Firefox plug-in which gives you SEO information
15. **Privacypartners.**com---IP address changing service
16. **HideMyAss**.com---Another IP address changing software.
17. **Matt Cutts Blog**---Matt Cutts is the voice of Google as far as SEO and is the lead engineer at Google for its web spam team.

Chapter 18
Tips and Tricks for Your Website

This last chapter I wrote for you to make sure you have a website that is not only SEO friendly, but human friendly too. After all, you are going through this entire process, to attract more customers and make more money. So if you have a website that looks like my 11 yr old brother built it, with broken links and overall does not look professional, you can drive traffic to it until you are blue in the face but most of that traffic may not buy from you.

Here are some things to keep in mind when building or re-designing your website:

1. What does the look and feel of the site say about your business?
2. Does the site have a clean design, or is there a lot of information everywhere?
3. How is it optimized for search engines?
4. How is the site optimized for visitors?
5. Do you have an irresistible offer for your visitors to get their contact information for further follow up?

(A free report, a coupon, something to entice them to give you their contact info?)
6. How does the site look in multiple browsers like Safari, Firefox, Internet Explorer, etc

In many sites, some of these areas can be greatly improved upon. If your current site is lacking in any areas you may want to consider re-designing it before embarking on your SEO campaign. If you do not yet have a website then great! You can start out with something good from the get go.
It is truly amazing to me how many people put up a website that does not look professional and expect people to treat them as professionals. Your website is your image and it should not be thrown up just to have one. I am actually guilty of the same thing, however, I recognized my mistake and got my site re-designed to look more professional and speak to the points I want people to know about my company when they visit the website.

Here are some tips to consider when building your website:

- **Navigation**---Make sure navigating through your site is easy and straight forward
- The most important information is **above the fold**-When someone first gets to your site, the first thing they see is the top of the page, so make sure the most important information you want them to know is here, since many people do not scroll down to the bottom to find the other important info you may have
- **Working links**---This is an obvious one, make sure you don't have any broken links hanging around.
- **Have a testimonials page**
- **Have a clean non-distracting design**

- **Have multiple ways to contact you**, make an appointment and so on
- **Trust factors-** Any badges you can put on your site like the BBB or Veri Sign, reputable associations you are a member of, etc
- **Video---**I strongly recommend the use on videos on your site since many people don't like to read boring text, but will watch a video, so make sure the video shows you as the only possible choice to do business with
- **Avoid too much flash-** as we discussed search engines cannot read flash as well, so you are losing space on your site that to them looks blank, which could have content with your keywords in it.
- **Have a lead capture system—**As mentioned above, you need to entice site visitors to give you their contact info, so make sure you have something set up. I could write a whole book on lead capture strategies, so for more information on this I suggest you do additional reading

I want to leave you with one last thought. There are 4 ways to make more money from your marketing, whether it is online or offline.

1. **Increase customers**
   - Increase traffic through SEO or PPC or both
   - Take out ads in print, TV or Radio
   - Do Events
   - Referrals (have a system in place for this)
   - Other marketing strategies

2. **Increase the Amount of Transactions per customer**

- Building your mailing and emailing list
- Sending out regular reminders of offers and promotions
- Offer up sells

3. **Increase average dollar amount per transaction**
   - Offer upgrades and reasons to purchase a higher package

4. **Decrease costs**
   - Increasing your conversion rates decreases costs. If you have a 1% conversion rate and you test and tweak thing so then you get a 2% conversion rate, that is double the sales with the same amount of traffic and advertising dollars being spent.
   - Buy traffic cheaper---if your Google ads convert better for example, they lower your cost per click. I'd say that is a huge incentive to constantly test and upgrade your conversion rates across the board

I added this last part to the book because it is not just about ranking high for profitable terms. Obviously that is important, but what you are really looking to do is probably drive sales and increase your bottom line. SEO can help, but you need to convert your site visitors to make sure your SEO campaign or any other online campaign is actually profitable.

References:

1. www.evolt.org/how_to_get_listed_in_**dmoz**
2. *www.PerpetualTrafficFormula.com*
3. The Art of SEO –by Eric Enge, Stephan Spencer, Rand Fishkin, Jessie Stricchiola
4. www.en.wikipedia.org

Glossary

Alt Tag---The ALT attribute is designed to be a description for images on HTML pages.

Anchor text---This is the visible, clickable text in a hyperlink.

Article resource box---The part of an article which credits the author who wrote it along with their website.

Back links---also known as inbound links, incoming links, inward links or inlinks, are incoming links to a website or web page.

BB Code--- BBCode or Bulletin Board Code is a lightweight markup language used to format posts in many message boards.

Conversion---A conversion is when a site visitor takes an action desired by the website owner such as making a purchase, signing up for a newsletter or downloading something.

Conversion rate---This is the number of visitors who take a desired action by the site owner on a website.

Google Adwords---Adwords is Google's pay per click advertising platform which allows advertisers to bid on keywords people are searching in Google's search engine.

IP address--- An IP address is a unique number that every computer connected to the internet is assigned. IP stands for internet protocol.

Keywords---Words or phrases being targeted in an SEO campaign.

Keyword Tag---A tag on an HTML website or page which describes the page by keywords related to that page.

Link building---A process in an SEO campaign to get incoming links to a particular website or set of websites.

Link Farms--- a link farm is any group of web sites that all hyperlink to every other site in the group. Although some link farms can be created by hand, most are created through automated programs and services.

Long tail keywords---Phrases of an SEO campaign consisting of between two and five words, usually used when searching for a rather specific item.

Meta tag---The description tag on a website which tells search engines in 160 or less what the page is about. The meta description is the also the text that appears on web results in a search engine.

Page rank--- A link analysis algorithm, named after Larry Page and used by the Google Internet search engine, that assigns a numerical weighting to each element of a hyperlinked set of documents, such as the World Wide Web, with the purpose of "measuring" its relative importance within the set.

PPC- Stands for pay per click and it is an advertising model where the advertiser pays a certain amount of money for every click they receive on an ad.

SEM---Stands for search engine marketing and it is the act of using search engines like Google and Yahoo to market products or services.

SEO---Stands for search engine optimization and it is the process of optimizing a website to rank higher for a particular term or terms within popular search engines like Google or Yahoo.

Title tags---Technically called title elements, define the title of a document and are required for all HTML/XHTML documents. It is one of the most important on page ranking factors in an SEO campaign.

Special Opportunity for Readers of This Book

Thank you very much for taking the time out of your busy schedule to read this book. I hope you found it useful and I hope you have started to or will put the strategies covered in this book to use for your online site. However, many of you may not have the time to implement this stuff, as it is very time consuming. Therefore if you would like to have Wizard Media help with your SEO campaign, here is a special opportunity just for you!

For you I will:

• Do complete Keyword research as described in this book with keyword recommendations on the terms you should focus on first
• Do complete website analysis with recommendations on changes to make your site more SEO friendly
• Do competition analysis for the top terms you need to target
• Make SEO recommendations to outrank your competitors

This will help you have the SEO road map you need to get started in your campaign with the right keywords you need to target, complete analysis of your main competitors and immediate changes you need to make to your site to beat them.

You get all this for just

$250 (Typically I charge $499 for this service).

This is your SEO Roadmap and will save you the mistake of choosing the wrong keywords or not optimizing your website correctly. To get started just fill out the form on the following page and email the information to: info@wizardmedia.net.

Or fill out the form located on our website under "SEO Sign Up" and mention this book to get the discounted rate.

SEO Form

Name:

Company Name:

Phone

Email:

Website:

How old is it?

Number of pages within the site:

Is the website built with a CMS system? (ex. Wordpress, Joomla, Drupal)

Do all of your pages have unique URLs?

Can the content on your website be found anywhere else online? This includes sister websites, articles, press releases, blogs, or anywhere else index-able by the search engines?

Can you add additional content to your website and/or additional pages of content to your website if necessary?

Who are your competitors? List top 3 at least.

In an effort to optimize your primary pages and avoid additional page and content creation, please list at least the top five pages on your website you would like to see ranking high in the search engines?

Do you have Google Analytics installed?

Have you had any SEO work done, especially link building to your knowledge?

(For Local Businesses) What cities do you want to target for your SEO campaign?

Main services you want to market with this SEO campaign?

What are the top 10 or 20 keywords you would like to target, or keywords you think your customers would type to find you?

1	14.
2 .	15.
3.	16.
4.	17.
5.	18.
6.	19.
7.	20.
8.	
9.	
10.	
11.	
12.	
13.	

Made in the USA
Lexington, KY
15 August 2015